Encyclopedia of Individual Work Related Personality Traits, Attitudes, and Behaviours: Understanding People at Workplace.

DR.NOOR UN NISA

DR. MUHAMMAD NAWAZ BALOCH

Introduction

This book is comprised of three major elements associated with an individual's personality, which include Traits, Attitudes and Behaviours. More specifically author tried to address these elements under the work-related domain. However, due to the identical and interrelated nature of elements related to personality traits, attitude and behaviour author could not categorize each element under a distinct label. In this book, the authors tried to define most of the personality traits, attitudes and behaviour related to work with the help of internet sources, literature and authors' understanding. This book works as an encyclopedia to search different personality traits, attitudes and behaviours and will be useful and helpful for new researchers to identify them and explore them further.

Personality has been found to be an essential element in personality research, particularly when it comes to predicting work-related performance and relationships at the workplace. Personality is a characteristic that distinguishes one person from another (Beer & Brooks, 2011) and indicates how a person will perform a given task in comparison to others (Sackett et al., 2002).

Attitude refers to a person's mental approach regarding the way an individual perceives, thinks, or feels about someone or something. **Behaviour** is a practical approach that includes the actions, moves, conduct or functions of an individual or group towards others. Furthermore, according to Denissen et al., 2011; Gerber et al., 2011; Myers, 1998), **personality traits** are regarded to be stable and steady throughout one's work life in a personality behaviour model.

1. Personality Related Theories

There are some personality theories that have been deemed major theories in the literature related to personality study, as stated by Awadh and Wan Ismail (2012), which includes.

1. Psychoanalytic theories.

2. Humanistic theories.

3. Biological theories.

4. Behavioural, Social learning and Cognitive theories; and

5. Trait theories.

Trait theory is one of the most widely accepted and influential personality theories, capturing the key elements that have a strong proclivity to contribute to specific behaviours. The differences in a person's tendency to form a consistent pattern of feelings, thoughts, and behaviours are determined by traits (Myers, 1998). Mount and Barrick (1998) identified the following gaps; since then, researchers have been trying to address this, but due to its extreme subjective nature not been achieved yet. Which says:

- There are hundreds of personality-related elements that have been investigated and/or are currently being investigated. This large number may make it difficult to organize and categorize all elements.

- There are a lot of similarities found in personality-related elements because Identical features have been described differently in several cases, resulting in similar traits with the same description but distinct labels. This even makes it difficult for the researcher to choose specific according to their research nature.

2. Employee's Work-Related Attitudes

In all organizational psychology, job attitudes are one of the oldest, most popular, and most influential fields of study. Employees gain professional experience during their job years; thus, this professional experience shapes the employee's attitude toward work and the way he or she approaches to perform their work, maintains relationships and reacts to any challenge.

Professional experience is not defined by the number of years a person has worked or the number of jobs they have done; rather, it is defined by the expertise and abilities that a professional has used to successfully execute a job. The employee's approach to addressing the problem and providing the way to execute the task is influenced by their 'experience.'

This book has been developed to test and identify the variety of employees' personal traits, professional traits, and work-related attitudes and behaviours at a workplace with the help of the literature available.

3. Psychological Withdrawal Behaviours

When people's work environments become stressful, they typically seek to detach or withdraw mentally. Although their bodies are present, their thoughts are elsewhere. Psychological withdrawal behaviours include daydreaming or talking with coworkers about non-work-related issues (Hulin, 1991; Lehman and Simpson, 1992).

4. Antagonistic Work Attitude

When you have a negative, antagonistic attitude confrontational attitude, you'll get more nasty comments and personal attacks. Unwillingness to labour extra hours or remain late for no cause. A refusal to "go the additional mile" while pushing others to do the same. While workplaces can foster beneficial, prosocial activity, they can also be a source of conflict and discord. Workplace actions such as bickering with coworkers or gossiping would be considered antagonistic. Anti-political work behaviours appear to have a positive correlation with political behaviour (Cheng, 1983; Randall et al., 1994).

5. Contentious Attitude and Personality

Contentious means **having a combative or confrontational attitude is what it means to be contentious.** Someone who enjoys arguing or fighting is said to be contentious. A contentious issue is one that is likely to spark debate. Some topics are extremely divisive. They're also contentious because people tend to argue about them, and the debates are likely to go on indefinitely. Argumentativeness, combativeness, disputatiousness, litigiousness, and scrappiness are all qualities or states of being contentious.

6. Acrimonious Behaviour

When a person uses bitter and harsh language and adopts a caustic demeanour, demeanour, or speech, employees may experience some mental health consequences at work because of acrimonious behaviours that range from low verbal-physical aggressiveness/low verbal-behavioural warmth to overt verbal-physical aggression.

7. Counterproductive Work Behaviour

Employees' willful and intentional behaviours that have the potential to harm a company and its members or both are referred to as counterproductive work behaviour (CWB) (Spector & Fox, 2005). Counterproductive work behaviours cover a wide range of topics. There was a lot of research done on individual counterproductive behaviours in the workplace prior to the early 1980s, and there is a number of factors associated with it, such as employee theft, pilferage, sabotage, slow and sloppy performance, tardiness, and absenteeism (Adler, and Althiede, 1978, Bensman and Gerver 1963; Cressey, 1953; Gouldner, 1954; Henry, 1978; Horning, 1970; Mars, 1973, Taylor and Walton, 1971).

8. Willful Behaviours

Acts that are purposeful, conscious, voluntary, and aimed to achieve a certain result are referred to as willful behaviour. The definition of the term "willful" varies depending on the context. Acts that are deliberate, cognizant, and aimed at achieving a goal are referred to as purposeful, conscious, and directed acts. Some intentional behaviour that has unintended or unfavourable consequences is labelled "hardheaded," "stubborn," or even "malicious."

9. Willful Ignorance or Willful Blindness/Choice Blindness

Willful ignorance refers to intentionally remaining unknown about anything; in other words, it is bad faith decision to avoid getting aware of something in order to avoid having to make unfavourable decisions as a result of that information. Purposeful Blindness with a purpose or blindness with a purpose (sometimes called "ignorance of the law," "willful ignorance," "contrived ignorance," "intentional ignorance," or "Nelsonian knowledge").

* Nelsonian knowledge (Uncountable) Knowledge that is credited to someone who was willfully ignorant of that knowledge and should have known it.

10. Self-Deception

The process of dismissing or reasoning away the relevance, significance, or importance of opposing evidence and logical argument is known as self-deception. Self-deception is defined as persuading oneself of a truth (or lack of truth) while concealing one's self-awareness of the deceit. Self-deception is described as the act of deceiving oneself or convincing oneself of something that is not true. According to psychologist Albert Bandura, "people avoid doing activities that they have an idea might reveal what they do not want to know" in real self-deception (2001, p. 16). 'Intentional ignorance is a deliberate act of self-deception, a willful embrace of ignorance,' says Nancy Tuana (2006, p. 11).

11. Antisocial Work Behaviours

Antisocial work behaviours are actions that show a lack of concern for the organization's and/or its members' interests and needs (Aquino & Douglas, 2003). They are intentional, norm-breaking activities by members of an organization that have the potential to harm the organization and/or its constituents (Bennett & Robinson, 2000, 2003; Fox & Spector, 1999; Robinson & Greenberg, 1998).

12. Norm-Violating Behaviours

When behaviour deviates from the norm and is regarded as deviant or unsuitable to the norm, it is said to be norm violating behaviour. Norm violations are defined as actions that violate one or more rules or principles of proper behaviour. Any action that infringes on a norm, whether informal (i.e., learnt through seeing others) or formal (i.e., written), is defined as a norm violation.

13. Moral Justification

The act of approving or rationalizing unethical behaviour is known as moral justification. In this way, moral justification is akin to Sykes and Matza's (1957) strategies of neutralization, which say that reasons for deviance may be valid to the deviant but not to society as a whole (p. 666). According to Sykes and Matza's depiction of the moral justification process, a person who engages in harmful behaviour makes it personal and socially acceptable by framing it as serving a cherished standard (Bandura et al., 1996). According to these three writers, moral disengagement, of which moral justification is a component, is theorized to have a direct impact on moral choice-making and has been linked to immoral decision making.

14.Social Inclusion

The process of improving the terms on which individuals and groups participate in society is known as social inclusion. It is the process of working to ensure that everyone, regardless of their background, has the opportunity to reach their greatest potential in life. It is also about Policies and initiatives that encourage equal access to (public) services as well as citizen participation in decision-making processes that affect their lives are examples of such efforts.

15.Social Exclusion

The term "social exclusion" refers to a scenario in which not everyone has equal access to the opportunities and services that enable them to live a decent and happy life. This includes not being able to contribute to the rules of the society in which they live or have their opinion heard. Infrastructure — even basic things like electricity and running water – and services like public education, healthcare, and the social welfare system are examples of inaccessible possibilities and services.

16.Social Cohesion

Social cohesiveness is a related notion that, in many ways, resembles social integration. All groups in a socially cohesive society have a sense of belonging, involvement, inclusion, acknowledgement, and validity. Demographically, such civilizations are not always homogeneous. Rather, they harness the potential of their societal variety through valuing difference (in terms of ideas, opinions, skills, etc.). As a result, when diverse interests intersect, they are less likely to fall into negative patterns of tension and conflict.

17. Workplace Deviance

"Voluntary behaviour that breaches significant organizational standards and thereby undermines the well-being of an organization, its members, or both" is how workplace deviance is characterized (Robinson & Bennett, 1995, p. 556). Deviant behaviour is fueled by interpersonal treatment (Robinson & Greenberg, 1998). Frustration, injustices, and threats to one's own safety are all common workplace experiences that lead to employee deviance (Bennett & Robinson, 2003). According to Ashforth (1997), abusive monitoring leads to feelings of irritation, helplessness, and alienation. Workplace deviance, in group psychology, may be described as the deliberate desire to cause harm to an organization – more specifically, a workplace. The concept has become an instrumental component in the field of organizational communication. Workplace deviance behaviours are **acts based on intentions to cause damage, discomfort, or punishment to the organization or other individuals within the organization**. Deviant behaviours can include smaller offences like intentionally working slower or could be as drastic as sabotage of work. (theft, fraud, sexual harassment, and destroying the property of the company).

18. Ostracism

Ostracism happens in a range of life areas, including organizational environments, and is characterized as being ignored or excluded by another individual or group of individuals (Williams, 2007). (Ferris et al., 2008; Fox & Stallworth, 2005). "The extent to which a person thinks that he or she is neglected or excluded by others in the office" is how workplace ostracism is defined (Williams, 2001). Ostracism actions in the workplace include critical withholding information, giving "the quiet treatment," avoiding talks or eye contact, and giving "the cold shoulder." A number of studies in psychology, sociology, and education (Gruter & Masters, 1986; Leary et Al., 2003; Twenge et al., 2001) have converged to support the idea that ostracism is a powerful, distinct, and pervasive social phenomenon.

19.Social Exchange Perspective

According to social exchange theory, a person will assess the cost (bad outcome) of a social engagement against the benefit (positive outcome). These expenses and benefits can be monetary, time-based, or in the form of service. The social exchange theory is a sociological and psychological theory that investigates the social behaviour of two parties who use a cost-benefit analysis to assess risks and rewards.

20.Dysfunctional Work Behaviours

Dysfunctional conduct is classified as antisocial behaviour, which is defined as "any behaviour that causes or intends to cause harm to a company, its employees, or stakeholders" (Giacalone and Greenberg, 1997, p. vii). Dysfunctional workplace behaviour indicates behaviour that deviates significantly from established workplace norms, which can be detrimental to overall organizational effectiveness. Workplace deviance, theft, hostility, violence, dishonesty, terrorism, and sabotage are examples of dysfunctional behaviours (Van Fleet & Griffin, 2006).

21. Workplace Sabotage

Workplace sabotage is behaviour intended to ''damage, disrupt, or subvert the organization's operations for the personal purposes of the saboteur by creating unfavourable publicity, embarrassment, delays in production, damage to property, the destruction of working relationships, or the harming of employees or customers'' (Crino, 1994, p. 312). According to a study from the University of British Columbia, managers should keep their teams connected and engaged in order to avoid workplace sabotage. "People who are envious of their coworkers try to bring them down by spreading negative rumours, withholding useful information, or secretly sabotaging their work," says Prof. Aquino, who collaborated on the study with colleagues from the University of Minnesota, Clemson University in South Carolina, and Georgia State University. Envy, on the other hand, according to Aquino, is merely fuel for sabotage. "Employees must experience 'moral disengagement,' a state of mind that permits people to rationalize or justify harming others, according to psychologists." The University of British Columbia. (2011, October 7). Workplace sabotage is fueled by envy, unleashed by disengagement.

22. Violent Behaviour

Any act or threat of physical violence, harassment, intimidation, or other threatening disruptive behaviour that occurs at work is referred to as workplace violence. Threats and verbal abuse are common, as are physical attacks and even homicide. Employees, clients, consumers, and visitors may be affected and involved. Workplace violence is described as violent acts directed against workers and others in the workplace, including both actual assaults and threats of physical harm (Centers for Disease Control and Prevention, 1996). (Olszewski, Parks, & Chikotas, 2007) divided the definition of workplace violence into four types of sources:

Type 1: Criminals who enter the workplace to commit a crime to commit violent crimes.

Type 2 acts of violence are those performed by people who are the recipients of workplace services.

Type 3—previous employees' violence against coworkers or management.

Type 4: workplace violence perpetrated by a non-employee who has a personal relationship with a worker.

Another source type of workplace violence is horizontal violence. According to Baltimore (2006), "Horizontal violence includes a wide range and variable degrees of antagonism: gossiping, criticism, innuendo, scapegoat, undermining, intimidation, passive aggression, withholding information, insubordination, bullying, and verbal and physical aggression" (p. 30).

23.Productive Work Behaviour

In an organization, productive behaviour is described as employee activities that contribute to the achievement of organizational goals and objectives (Britt & Jex, 2008). In the workplace, productive behaviour is defined as behaviour that promotes results or meets objectives. Productive behaviours can be measured using performance indicators like output, work quality, and other benchmarks.

24.Prosocial Organizational behaviour

Cooperating with coworkers, taking action when necessary to protect the organization from unexpected danger, suggesting ways to improve the organization, deliberate self-development and preparation for higher levels of organizational responsibility, and speaking favourably about the organization to outsiders are examples of prosocial behaviour. Prosocial behaviour includes acts such as assisting, sharing, donating, cooperating, and volunteering. They are constructive social behaviours that develop and sustain other people's well-being and integrity. A number of behavioural and social scientists focused their attention on these behaviours in the 1960s and early 1970s (Berkowitz & Daniels, 1963; Campbell, 1965; Gouldner, 1960; Latane & Darley, 1970).

25.Employee's Innovative Behaviour

Employee innovation behaviour is defined as behaviour related to the development of new products, the development of new markets, or the improvement of business routines within their organization. Innovative behaviour can be defined as the "intentional generation, promotion, and realization of new ideas within a work role, group, or organization" (Scott and Bruce 1994). The introduction and application of new ideas, products, processes, and procedures to a person's job function, work unit, or organization is referred to as innovative behaviour. Persons or groups of individuals inside an organization can engage in innovative behaviour. It comprises several behaviours associated with the invention, promotion, and implementation of new ideas and is a larger term than creativity. (Yuan and Marquardt, 2021).

26. Inclusive Leadership

"Words and deeds by a leader or leaders that express an invitation and gratitude for others' efforts," defined Nembhard and Edmondson (2006: 947). Coming to the table at whatever level, being a respected participant, and being completely accountable for your contribution to the best results is what the word inclusive means. The principle that 'everyone matters' (Roberson, 2006) with their access to knowledge and resources won out in this inclusion (Mor-Barak & Cherin, 1998). The term "inclusive leadership" was coined by Nembhard and Edmondson (2006), who argued that an inclusive leader creates an environment where "voices are actually respected" (p. 948).

27. Proactive Behaviour

Parker, Williams, and Turner (2006) discovered that proactive conduct, defined as self-initiated and future-oriented action aimed at changing and improving one's circumstances or self, contributes to a variety of positive work outcomes (Bindl & Parker, 2010). Proactivity, also known as proactive behaviour, is self-initiated conduct that aims to fix an issue before it arises. Acting in advance of a future circumstance, rather than reacting, is what proactive action entails. Proactive workplace behaviour can be defined as a "process whereby individuals recognize potential problems or opportunities in their work environment and self-initiate change to bring about a better future work situation" (Parker and Collins, 2010, p. 636).

28. Impostor Syndrome (IS)

Clinical psychologists Pauline Clance and Suzanne Imes coined the term "Impostor Phenomenon" to describe impostor syndrome in their 1978 paper. The term 'phenomenon' rather than syndrome still dominates psychological literature, and the condition is not classified as a mental disorder in the Diagnostic and Statistical Manual of the American Psychiatric Association. C. Imposter syndrome is a condition in which you distrust your own talents and feel like a fraud. It adversely impacts high-achieving individuals who struggle to accept their achievements. Individuals who suffer from the Impostor Phenomenon have strong feelings that their accomplishments are unjustified, and they are concerned that they will be revealed as frauds (Sakulku & Alexander, 2011). The Impostor Phenomenon refers to an "internal experience of intellectual phoniness" (Matthews & Clance, 1985, p. 71) in individuals who are highly successful but unable to internalize their success (Bernard, Dollinger, & Ramaniah, 2002; Clance & Imes, 1978). Clance believed that the Impostor Phenomenon is not "a pathological disease that is inherently self-damaging or self-destructive" (Clance, 1985, p. 23). Rather, it interferes with the psychological well-being of a person (Sakulku & Alexander, 2011).

29.Perfectionism

In psychology, perfectionism is a broad personality style characterized by a person's concern with aiming for flawlessness and perfection, as well as critical self-judgements and concerns about other people's evaluations. Perfectionism is generally defined as a desire to be or appear perfect or even to believe that perfection is possible. It's usually regarded as a strength rather than a weakness. The term "healthy perfectionism" is sometimes used to characterize or defend perfectionistic behaviour. Hamachek (1978) proposed about 30 years ago that there are two types of perfectionism: one that is positive "normal perfectionism" and a negative form labelled "neurotic perfectionism." perfectionism was defined as "demanding of oneself or others a higher quality of performance than is required by the situation."

* Neurotic perfectionists are prone to setting unreasonable goals and become unhappy when they are unable to achieve them.
* Normal perfectionists are more likely to strive for perfection without jeopardizing their self-esteem, and they enjoy the process.

30.Employee Silence Behaviour

Pinder & Harlos (2001) defined organizational silence as "withholding genuine expression about behavioural, cognitive, and/or effective evaluations of organizational circumstances from people who appear capable of changing the situation, with a focus on individual employee silence as a reaction to injustice". Employee silence refers to circumstances in which employees, whether intentionally or accidentally, suppress information that could be valuable to the organization of which they are apart. If employees do not speak up to a supervisor or management, this can happen. Prior research has shown that employee silence is systematically predicted by a variety of individual actors, such as power distance, proactive personality, and perceived organizational politics (Lam & Xu, 2019; Morrison et al., 2015; AL-Abrrow, 2018), as well as work environment conditions, such as workplace ostracism, abusive supervision, and organizational justice (e.g., Lam & Xu, 2019; Morrison et al., 2015; AL (Jahanzeb & Fatima, 2018; Kiewitz et al., 2016; Whiteside & Barclay, 2013).

31. Unconscious Behaviours

Unconscious, also known as "Subconscious, is a complex mental activity that occurs within an individual without his knowledge. Sigmund Freud, the father of psychoanalysis, believed that unconscious processes might influence a person's behaviour even if he is unable to report on them". Suppressed feelings, auto-responses, complexes, and hidden phobias are examples of unconscious happenings. One type of unconscious action is when we actively choose to do something, but then the unconscious takes over and allows us to complete the activity without conscious supervision. Even more intriguing is another type of unconscious activity. These are actions that we knowingly engage in but are oblivious to why we do so (Wheeler, 2015).

32. The Mum Effect

"Mum effect, or "code of silence", is a situation when one or more persons decide to withhold information despite knowing that such option is unethical" (Ramingwong and Sajeev, 2013). The Mum effect happens due to several reasons. Yet, the most participate root behind this risk is defined as a fear of negative consequences which might arise after the information disclosure [3]. "The Mum effect," sometimes known as the "code of silence," occurs when one or more people choose to suppress information despite knowing that doing so is unethical" (Ramingwong and Sajeev, 2013). The mum effect occurs for a variety of causes. However, the most common cause of this risk is the fear of negative repercussions that may occur as a result of the information exposure. The mum effect is a significant risk that arises when a member of staff is hesitant to report unpleasant facts. It can take various forms, including withholding crucial information, failing to report concerns, and attempting to cover up for others' faults. One of the potential factors behind the mum effect is culture. People from various cultural backgrounds are anticipated to react to this risk in different ways.

Interestingly, a study showed no significant variations in postgraduate students' hesitation to disclose concerns to their supervisors between Eastern European, Western European, and Asian students. To support this hypothesis, a larger group of people would need to be studied.

33. Post-Pandemic Syndrome/ Post-Pandemic Stress Disorder

According to O'Kane, symptoms of PPSD are similar to PTSD and can vary from person to person. These might include increased "anxiety, low motivation, feeling hopeless or powerless, disrupted sleep, changes in appetite, feeling numb, being increasingly angry or irritated, negative or catastrophic thinking, withdrawing socially, feelings of struggling to cope" and feeling like "I can't be bothered with anything, particularly during Covid-19 then more likely you are suffering from PPSD." So, If you were functioning well before the pandemic and are now experiencing these symptoms, it is likely you are experiencing PPSD."

34. Overdone Strength

Stop Overdoing Your Strengths is a term coined by Bob Kaplan and Rob Kaiser in 2009 to describe the phenomenon of overdoing your strengths. This is when we use a particular area of expertise too intensely or at the wrong time, resulting in negative side effects (Kaplan and Kaiser, 2009).

35. Workplace Spirituality

Spirituality in the workplace is a movement that began in the early 1920s. It emerged as a grassroots movement with individuals seeking to live their faith and/or spiritual values at work. Workplace spirituality has been defined as "a framework of organizational values evidenced in the culture that promotes employees' experience of transcendence through the work process, facilitating their sense of being connected to others in a way that provides feelings of completeness and joy" (Giacalone & Jurkiewicz, 2003). Pawar (2008) defined workplace spirituality as "employee experiences of self-transcendence, meaning, and community in the workplace and it also acknowledges that these experiences could come from various mechanisms including organizational ones."

36.Insider Threat Behaviour Detection

Insider threat behaviour at work refers to the risk of an insider, either intentionally or unintentionally, abusing his or her allowed access to compromise the organization's security. This threat can include espionage, terrorism, unlawful disclosure of security information, or the loss or deterioration of corporate, contract, or program information, resources, or capabilities, among other things. By categorizing potential risk indicators, insider threat programs assist organizations in detecting and identifying persons who may become insider threats. These indicators are behaviours that are both observable and reportable, and they suggest people who may be on the verge of becoming a threat.

37.Love Bombing

"Love bombing" is a frequent manipulation method used by narcissistic employers to keep their employees under control. Love bombing is when narcissists lavish excessive praise and affection on their victims to exert control over them. Love bombing is a method of influencing someone by displays of care and attention. It can be used in a variety of ways, both positively and negatively. Love bombing has been highlighted as a probable aspect of a cycle of abuse by psychologists, who have warned against it.

38. Dark Triad Personality/Leadership

In psychology, the dark triad comprises some negative elements of personality traits which include narcissism, Machiavellianism, and psychopathy. They are called dark because of their malevolent qualities. The common core of all three Dark Triad traits is social aversion, emotional coldness, aggressiveness, and a tendency to manipulate others (Paulhus & Williams, 2002). Dark triad leaders are either praised as visionaries and role models, or they can destroy entire companies – or something in between. Many of their problematic characteristics (e.g., self-confidence, grandiosity, an exploitative nature, and persistence) can also make the dark triad personalities successful.

39. Light Triad Personality

The "light triad" — the characteristics of a loving person who is concerned about others — was recently identified by experts. According to the experts, recognizing these characteristics brings much-needed attention to our positive side. The light triangle, according to Dr Kaufman and colleagues, comprises Kantianism, humanism, and confidence in mankind. When we see individuals as means to themselves rather than means to a goal, we are practising Kantianism. We're not looking to exploit them in any way. It's the polar opposite of Machiavellianism, and it's founded on Immanuel Kant's philosophy. Humanism is the value placed on the dignity and worth of each human. When we feel that humans are basically good, we have faith in mankind.

40. Behaviour of Relational Justice

In a post-conflict environment, relational justice (RJ) is described as justice achieved by cooperative behaviour, agreement, negotiation, or communication among actors. In relationships, a type of social justice defines how fairness is produced and maintained between individuals.

41. Workplace Ostracism

The term "workplace ostracism" was coined to describe situations in which individuals were ostracized, disregarded, or dismissed by their coworkers. Ostracism at work is a form of "cold aggression." Furthermore, workplace ostracism is seen as "social death", according to Li 2021. Workplace ostracism, which is defined as "the extent to which a person thinks that he or she is neglected or excluded by others" (Ferris et al., 2008, p. 1348), can have serious effects on both organizations and individuals (Howard et al., 2020). The management literature has extensively examined the effects of workplace ostracism on victims Mao et al. (2018), Williams (2007), Wu et al. (2011). In a social framework, an individual who is ostracized by another party (e.g., coworkers or superiors) may suffer injury, loss, or misfortune (Aquino and Lamertz, 2004).

42. Resourcefulness Skills

The skill and ingenuity to deal with challenging situations or uncommon challenges are defined as resourcefulness. It's all about problem-solving and completing tasks despite hurdles and limits. "A person's capacity to find efficient and innovative solutions to problems is referred to as resourcefulness". Being resourceful also entails making the most of your resources to create something new or better. This ability to adapt and solve challenges in novel ways could help you land a job.

43. Psychological/ Mental Wellbeing

"Employee wellbeing is defined as the overall mental, the physical, emotional, and economic health of your employees. It's influenced by various factors such as their relationships with co-workers, the decisions they make, and the tools and resources they have access to" (Kundi, Aboramadan, Elhamalawi and Shahid, 2020).

Psychological well-being is a key component of overall happiness and has been linked to physical health, longer lives, and happier employees. A proactive approach to psychological well-being, rather than only risk management, is part of a positive approach to psychological well-being. At its most fundamental level, psychological wellbeing (PWB) is quite similar to other terminology that relates to good mental states, such as happiness or satisfaction, and it is not essential or beneficial to worry about fine distinctions between such terms in many aspects. Employee health and well-being appear to be one of the most important aspects influencing organizational success and performance, according to research (Bakker et al., 2019; Turban and Yan, 2016). A number of researches have shown that employee happiness leads to improved organizational performance and productivity (Hewett et al., 2018), customer satisfaction (Sharma et al., 2016), staff engagement (Tisu et al., 2020), and organizational citizenship behaviour (Tisu et al., 2020). (OCB; Mousa et al., 2020).

44. Work-Life Balance

Work-family balance is a term that refers to a well-integrated work and family life, as well as a condition in which the individual is actively engaged in both. The link between your employment and other essential things in your life, such as your family, sports and social life, domestic tasks, volunteer obligations, and so on, is known as work-life balance. You probably have a healthy work-life balance if you feel like you have adequate time for all of these things in your life. Work/Life Balance is a state of balance in which a person's employment and personal life responsibilities are balanced.

45. Psychological Capital

'Human capital is a word you've probably heard before. It refers to an organization's human resources, which include employees' skills, knowledge, and competencies. However, it's likely that you've never heard of psychological capital. Psychological capital is a set of resources that can be used to help a person improve their job performance and success. Self-efficacy, optimism, hope, and resilience are among the four resources included. This widely accepted fundamental idea of psychological capital, or simply PsyCap, is based on positive psychology and positive organizational behaviour (POB) in particular. Hope, efficacy, resilience, and optimism, or the HERO inside, are the first-order positive psychological resources that makeup PsyCap. These four are the most theory and research-based, positive, validly measurable, state-like, and have an impact on attitudes, behaviours, performance, and well-being (Luthans and Morgan, 2017).

46. Workplace Anxiety

Workplace anxiety refers to a sense of being stressed, nervous, uneasy, or tense about one's job, coworkers, or even public speaking. Workplace anxiety refers to a sense of being stressed, nervous, uneasy, or tense about one's job, coworkers, or even public speaking. Workplace anxiety is characterized as emotions of worry, unease, and tension over job-related performance, which is a response to stresses in the form of a strain symptom (Jex, 1998; McCarthy, Trougakos, & Cheng, 2016). Individual differences, as well as environmental influences, influence it (Motowidlo, Packard, & Manning, 1986), and it is operationalized at both the dispositional and situational levels. According to research, 40% of Americans experience anxiety throughout the workday (American Psychological Association, 2009), and 72% of those who experience everyday worry say it interferes with their work and personal lives (Anxiety and Depression Association of America, 2006).

*Workplace Phobic Anxiety: Job phobia is described as a phobic anxiety reaction that manifests as panic symptoms when one thinks about or approaches the workplace. People with workplace fear frequently avoid confrontation with coworkers and are frequently absent from work.

47. Work-Related Stress

Job stress is defined as the negative physical and emotional reactions that occur when the job demands do not meet the worker's capabilities, resources, or needs. Work-related stress is a reaction that people experience when they are confronted with work demands and pressures that are out of proportion to their knowledge and talents and which put their ability to cope to the test. "Workplace stress can be defined as a change in one's physical or mental state in reaction to workplaces that represent an appraised challenge or threat to that individual," according to research by Colligan and Higgins, 2005. According to the same research, a number of factors contribute to job stress. Toxic work environments, negative workloads, isolation, types of hours worked, role conflict, role ambiguity, lack of autonomy, career development barriers, difficult relationships with administrators and/or coworkers, managerial bullying, harassment, and organizational climate are just a few of these factors. If the stressors persist, the individual is in danger of developing physiological and psychological illnesses, which can lead to higher absenteeism, organizational dysfunction, and lower productivity. Managers can use intervention tactics to support and intervene with employees who are dealing with workplace stress (Colligan and Higgins, 2006).

48. Optimism Bias

Optimism bias is a cognitive bias that leads people to feel they are less likely to face a negative occurrence than they actually are. Unrealistic optimism or comparative optimism are some names for it. Our tendency to overestimate our chances of having pleasant events while underestimating our chances of experiencing negative events is known as the optimism bias. The optimism bias is the erroneous notion that our chances of experiencing bad occurrences are lower and our chances of experiencing happy events are higher than our peers'. The propensity to overestimate the chance of good future outcomes while underestimating the likelihood of unpleasant future outcomes is known as optimism bias (Irwin 1953; Weinstein 1980; Slovic, Fischoff, and Lichtenstein 1982; Slovic 2000).

49.Animal Spirits

"Animal spirits" is a term introduced by the famous British economist, John Maynard Keynes, to explain people's intention toward financial decisions regarding buying and selling securities in the situation of economic stress or uncertainty. Animal spirits reflect the feelings of optimism, fear, and pessimism, which can influence financial decision-making and, in turn, promote or stifle economic growth.

50.Crisis Ready

When your team is crisis ready, they don't merely deal with a problem or crisis; they instinctively solve it. Managing it in a way that fosters greater trust, credibility, and goodwill among the people who matter most to your company. The process of responding to and averting future crises in an organization is known as crisis ready leadership. By providing emotional support, most crisis leaders emphasize the needs of their employees and customers.

51. Invincibility Fable

David Elkind was the first to propose this habit, which is a type of egocentric thinking that is uniquely found in teenagers (1967). Invincibility is a stage of adolescent development that has been linked to risky conduct. It causes kids to have feelings like: "Every experience is unique," "Nothing happens to anyone else as it does to me," and "Nothing happens to anybody else like it does to me." No one can understand what I'm going through because my experiences/feelings are unique. Nothing awful is going to happen to me; accidents happen to other people. The invincibility fable is a thought pattern that has been observed in a large number of people. It is an egocentric way of thinking that is characterized by a conviction of indestructibility, that they won't get caught while doing wrong and that they won't be wounded (or killed) by indulging in risky actions.

52. Workplace Individuality/ Individualism

Individual work refers to the act of accomplishing duties on one's own. Working alone helps you to concentrate on what you want or need to get a job done. The notion behind boosting individuality is that people are more likely to like their jobs if they feel encouraged and have the freedom to accomplish their jobs how they want. Employees that are happy in their jobs are more inclined to work harder for the organization.

* Individualism advocates a self-directed, autonomous, and self-contained vision of the individual. Individualism is defined as a self-centred attitude, a focus on self-sufficiency and control, the pursuit of

individual goals that may or may not be consistent within-group goals, a willingness to confront members of the in-group to which they belong, and a culture in which people take pride in their own achievements.

53. Workplace Conformity

In the workplace, conformity refers to observing workplace standards as well as sticking to established or socially anticipated company practices and processes. Employees are expected to adapt to company norms and standards and execute job functions using traditional business procedures, which is commonly termed conformity. Conformity gets a bad rap because of people like these. In today's business, successful conformity does not imply restricting uniqueness or pushing individuals to follow cultural norms. Instead, conformance entails establishing guidelines for how personnel are expected to accomplish their tasks. Social conformity is a type of social influence that results in a change of behaviour or belief in order to fit in with a group. The two types of social conformity are normative conformity and informational conformity. Normative conformity occurs because of the desire to be liked and accepted.

54. Diffusion of Responsibility

The term "diffusion of responsibility" refers to the fact that when the number of spectators grows, the individual bystander's sense of personal responsibility diminishes. When those who need to make a decision wait for someone else to act instead, this is known as diffusion of responsibility. The larger the group, the more likely it is that each person will do nothing, believing that someone else in the group will respond. People who are relieved of duty feel less compelled to act because they believe, correctly or mistakenly, that someone else will. When we don't feel responsible for a situation, we don't feel as bad about doing little to help.

55.Self-Monitoring

Self-monitoring is a personality attribute that involves the ability to keep track of and regulate one's own appearances, feelings, and behaviours in response to social situations. It entails being conscious of your actions and how they affect your surroundings. Self-monitoring is defined by Snyder (1974) as the degree to which people monitor, adjust, and control their behaviour based on how others perceive it. Self-monitoring is really about "status-oriented impression management goals" (Gangestad & Snyder, 2000; p. 547). Socially ambitious, high self-monitors have a great desire to portray positive images of themselves in order to impress others.

* High self-monitors are constantly scanning the social climate around them and adapting their behaviour to fit the circumstances. As a result, high self-monitors are more likely to engage in behaviours that will help them gain acceptance and/or status (Gangestad & Snyder, 2000; Turnley & Bolino, 2001).

*Low self-monitors, on the other hand, associate image improvement in social contexts with little psychological significance. Self-monitor is more important to them than status or reputation. They place a strong emphasis on remaining loyal to themselves and their essential values and ideas. They are less willing to provide misleading pictures in social situations since their behaviour is not impacted by how others see them (Day & Kilduff, 2003; Gangestad & Snyder, 2000).

56.Self-Efficacy

Self-efficacy is a person's belief in his or her ability to carry out the actions required to achieve specified performance goals (Bandura, 1977, 1986, 1997). Self-efficacy refers to one's belief in one's ability to control one's own motivation, behaviour, and social environment. There are two levels of self-efficacy: low and high. Self-efficacy comes from three different places. Enactive self-mastery is the most potent factor of self-efficacy, followed by role modelling and then verbal persuasion.

57.Self Esteem

Your overall view of yourself — how you feel about your strengths and limits — is referred to as self-esteem. When you have a healthy sense of self-esteem, you feel good about yourself and believe that you are worthy of others' regard. When you have poor self-esteem, you don't appreciate your own thoughts and opinions. Self-esteem is a person's subjective assessment of their own value. Self-esteem is made up of one's self-perceptions as well as emotional states, including triumph, despair, pride, and humiliation. Self-esteem is still one of the most widely studied topics in social psychology (Baumeister 1993; Mruk 1995; Wells & Marwell 1976; Wylie 1979). Self-esteem is generally thought of as a component of one's self-concept, although it is one of the most significant aspects of one's self-concept for some people. Indeed, for a time, self-esteem was given so much emphasis in the literature on the self that it seemed to be interchangeable with self-concept (Rosenberg 1976, 1979). Self-esteem is a term that relates to a person's overall favourable opinion of themselves (Gecas 1982; Rosenberg 1990; Rosenberg et al. 1995). There are two unique dimensions to it: skill and worth (Gecas 1982; Gecas & Schwalbe 1983). The competence dimension (efficacy-based self-esteem) refers to how capable and efficacious people believe they are. The worth dimension (worth-based self-esteem) refers to how much people believe they are valuable people.

58.Social Loafing

The "Ringelmann Effect," which describes the tendency for individuals to lower their productivity when in a group (Ringlemann, 1913), was renamed "social loafing" after Ingham, Levinger, Graves, and Peckham were successful in demonstrating individual effort declines in a curvilinear fashion when people work as a group or only believe they are working in a group (Ringlemann, 1913), (Ingham, Levinger, Graves, & Peckham, 1974). The psychological phenomenon of social loafing is when team members do less work in a group context. When people are judged as members of a group, they don't pull their own weight, according to the social loafing effect. Employees naturally lessen their effort when working in a group rather than alone, which is known as social loafing (Karau & Williams, 1993). Employee engagement and organizational effectiveness are both harmed as a result of social loafing.

59. Cyber Loafing

Employees who utilize their job-provided Internet access for personal purposes while appearing to do genuine work are known as cyberlockers. The phrase "cyberloafing" comes from the term "goldbricking," which originally meant "putting a gold coating on a worthless metal brick." Employee misuse of a company's Internet resources has gotten a lot of attention from organizational experts in recent years (Lim and Chen,2012). Employees who use their company's Internet access for non-work-related purposes during working hours have been referred to as cyberslacking or cyberloafing (Lim 2002). Cyberloafing was traditionally thought of as a sort of workplace production deviance by academics (e.g. Lim 2002, Lim and Teo 2005). This is because these cyber activities (browsing and emailing) that take place at work during working hours are a waste of time and divert employees' attention away from their responsibilities.

60. Locus of Control (Internal and External)

A person's perspective of the underlying fundamental causes of occurrences in his or her life is referred to as his or her locus of control. The locus of control is a psychological term that describes how firmly people believe they have control over the events and experiences that shape their life. The locus of control is crucial in determining how a person perceives his or her surroundings. While the locus of control contains motivational characteristics, it is more than that (Zigarmi et al., 2018). The locus of control is more concerned with who or what controls a person's results (Deci & Ryan, 1985). Individuals with an internal locus of control are more likely to feel that their acts influence the rewards or results of their actions (Mueller & Thomas, 2001). As a result, individuals are more likely to believe in their own abilities, skills, and effort. Such people are more likely to approach difficulties and hurdles in a good manner by employing constructive solutions (Luthans, Avey, Avolio, Norman, & Combs, 2006). As a result, they attain higher levels of success and demonstrate a drive to learn and improve their knowledge and abilities (Hsiao et al., 2016). As a result, their belief in their ability to influence outcomes (Mueller & Thomas, 2001) will make them more proactive and aware of entrepreneurial chances. Individuals with an external locus of control, on the other hand, believe that their benefits are out of their reach ((Hsiao et al., 2016). As a result, individuals are more likely to attribute personal gains or outcomes to external forces like luck (Ng et al., 2006).

61. Perception (Visual Perception/Social)

Individual perception is influenced by both our external and internal forces. The following are some well-known biases: Individuals do not view items in isolation when it comes to visual perception. We perceive visual features and then extrapolate them cognitively. In terms of perceptions, research has shown that how employees view their work environment has the greatest impact on their productivity. As a result, in order to influence productivity, businesses must examine how employees feel about their jobs, workplace, policies, and coworkers.

62. Cyber Slacking

Employees becoming distracted by technology in the workplace, mainly owing to personal, non-work-related Internet usage, is referred to as cyberslacking. Cyberslacking (also referred to as cyberloafing, non-work-related computing, cyber deviance, personal use at work, Internet abuse, workplace Internet leisure browsing, and junk computing) is the use of the Internet and mobile technology during work hours for personal purposes (Bock & Ho, 2009; Johnson & Indvik, 2004; Lim, 2002; Mastrangelo, Everton, & Jolton, 2006). (Bock & Ho, 2009; Johnson & Indvik, 2004; Lim, 2002; Mastrangelo, Everton, & Jolton, 2006). These behaviours appear to be widespread among computer-using professions: in recent research, employees reported spending at least 1 hour on non-work-related activities during a standard workday, with the Internet accounting for the majority of the nonwork-related time (Salary.com., 2009). Non-work-related activities such as online shopping, blogging, gaming, and instant messaging are common during working hours (Madden, 2009), as online gambling (Mills, Hu, Beldona, & Clay, 2001), pornography (Cooper, Safir, & Rosenmann, 2006), personal investing, and online auctions (Pee, Woon, & Kankanhalli, 2008) are also a source of concern. Eighty per cent of information workers acknowledged using a computer for personal email or messaging while on the job in one of the few nationwide studies on cyberslacking activities (Garrett & Danziger, 2008a; Garrett & Danziger, 2008b). range from $178 billion to $178 billion per year (Websense, 2006). In addition to the financial losses associated with decreased worker productivity, cyberslacking jeopardizes network security, places a strain on organizational capacity, and exposes businesses to lawsuits involving everything from securities fraud to sexual harassment (Oswalt, Elliott-Howard, & Austin, 2003).

63. Goldbricking

Goldbricking is the act of doing less work than one is capable of but still appearing to be productive. The word comes from the confidence trick of adding a gold coating on a worthless metal brick—while the worker appears to be hardworking on the surface, they are actually less valuable. The act of someone purposefully doing less work than they are capable of while convincing others that they are working to their full skill and capacity is known as goldbricking. The phrase's imagery illustrates a gold-painted brick that has been used to conceal itself and raise its value.

64. Leadership Behaviour

Leadership behaviour refers to the characteristics and behaviours that make a person effective as a leader. This is the process of a person leading, influencing, and guiding the work of others in order to attain specific objectives. These actions and methods can be taught to others in order to help them become more effective. In enterprises, leaders are crucial, and their actions have a significant impact on their employees' work behaviour, performance, and well-being (e.g., Avolio, Walumbwa, & Weber, 2009; Kuoppala, Lamminpää, Liira, & Vainio, 2008; Kuoppala, Lamminpää, Liira, & Vainio, 2008).

Popular leadership theories that highlighted one or two major behaviours led much of the research on the consequences of leader conduct. Early leadership theories emphasized task-oriented and relations-oriented behaviour, such as path-goal theory (House, 1971), leadership substitutes theory (Kerr & Jermier, 1978), situational leadership theory (Hersey & Blanchard, 1977), and the managerial grid (Blake & Mouton, 1964), and these meta-categories were used in much of the research conducted from 1960 to 1980. Much of the study on the consequences of leadership behaviour has been centred on transformational and charismatic leadership theories since the 1980s (Avolio, Bass, & Jung, 1999; Bass, 1985; Conger & Kanungo, 1987; House, 1977; Shamir, House, & Arthur, 1993).

65. Creative Behaviour

The creative act, or a group of acts, has been defined as conduct that makes the creative act explicit. It is a behaviour that allows one to engage freely in pursuit of self-expression, creation, research, design, and problem-solving, free of self- or externally imposed restraints. People who engage in creative conduct are at ease and free to identify themselves based on their own preferences rather than the opinions of others. Deferring judgment, taking responsibility for innovation, taking risks, and being open to new experiences are all examples of creative conduct. Lateral thinking, visual reading, out-of-the-box thinking, copywriting, artistic creativity, problem-solving, analytical mind, and divergent thinking are some of the best examples of creative thinking skills. Intentionally getting fresh insights and different ideas using current information is what creative thinking is all about. Often, creative thinking entails combining diverse ways of thinking and studying data from many perspectives in order to uncover new patterns.

66.Social Isolating Behaviour

Social isolation, which is the unwillingness or inability to discuss one's feelings with others, is a form of social isolation. Individuals who are socially isolated and lack emotional engagement and support may become emotionally numb or removed from their own feelings. The term "social isolation" usually refers to unwelcomed and harmful alone. People who are socially isolated may lack close friends or coworkers, and they may feel lonely or unhappy. They may have low self-esteem or be anxious. The term "social isolation" usually refers to unwelcomed and harmful alone. People who are socially isolated may lack close friends or coworkers, and they may feel lonely or unhappy. They may have low self-esteem or be anxious.

67.People-Pleasing Behaviour

People pleasers will go to any length to avoid disagreement, even if it means transforming into someone completely different. Your value is determined by how others perceive you. To feel good about themselves, people pleasers require external approval. They will go to great lengths to gain admiration from others. Dependent Personality Disorder is linked to a need to please. While the people-pleaser may not require others to perform tasks for them, they certainly require others. The Masochistic Personality type, which relates to Dependent Personality, is linked to the appealing personality. People-pleasing is linked to a personality trait called "sociotropy," which refers to a preoccupation with pleasing others and obtaining their approval in order to sustain relationships. This behaviour could be a sign of a mental health problem. Codependency and people-pleasing are the same things. People-pleasing is frequently a part of codependency; when you're in a codependent relationship, you put another person wants ahead of your own. It's almost as if codependency is a destructive form of people-pleasing.

68. Playful Behaviour/Playful Personality

Playfulness is a psychological attribute that manifests itself in different ways in different persons. "Boredom is a difficult thing to deal with for persons who are particularly lively. They have the ability to turn practically any mundane scenario into fun or personally engaging encounter, "Professor René Proyer, a psychologist at MLU, explains. In research and practice across fields, playfulness as a personality attribute in adults has been largely ignored. Amongst others, there are some outcomes positively related to playfulness, including "coping" (e.g., Staempfli, 2007; Magnuson and Barnett, 2013), "work performance and innovative behaviour at work" (Glynn and Webster, 1992; Yu et al., 2007), "creativity and intrinsic motivation" (Amabile et al., 1994; Proyer, 2012b), "virtuousness" (Proyer and Ruch, 2011), "sexual selection" (Chick et al., 2012; Proyer and Wagner, 2015), "academic success" (Proyer, 2011), "low expressions in the Impostor phenomenon" (Brauer and Proyer, 2017), or "subjective well-being" (Proyer, 2013, 2014a,b; Proyer et al., 2018a).

69. Extrovert and Introvert Personalities

Extrovert and introvert personalities behave quite differently in social environments. Extroverts prefer to seek out, participate in, and enjoy social contacts, whereas introverts are quiet and distant in social situations, often choosing to avoid them entirely. An introvert is a person who exhibits traits of the introverted personality type, which implies they prefer to focus on their inner thoughts and ideas rather than what is going on around them. Rather than in large groups or crowds, they prefer to spend time with one or two people. In a positive way, extroverts are generally described as talkative, gregarious, action-oriented, eager, friendly, and outgoing on the positive side. They are sometimes regarded as attention-seeking, easily distracted, and unable to spend time alone on the negative side.

70. Authoritarianism

The attitude of an individual toward authority is referred to as authoritarianism. More specifically, an authoritarian orientation is characterized by a strong belief that it is legitimate and appropriate for people to have distinct status and power differences. A high authoritarian, according to T. W. Adorno, is (1) demanding, directive, and controlling of her subordinates; (2) submissive and deferential toward superiors; (3) intellectually rigid; (4) fearful of social change; (5) highly judgmental and categorical in reactions to others; (6) distrustful; and (7) hostile in response to restraint. Nonauthoritarians, on the other hand, believe that power and status differences should be minimized, that social change can be beneficial, and that people should be more accepting of others and less judgmental.

These disparities can have huge ramifications in the workplace. Employees with a high level of authoritarianism, for example, perform better under strict supervisory control, whereas those with a lower level of authoritarianism do better under more participatory supervision, according to research.

71.Dogmatism

Dogmatism is a cognitive style characterized by closed-mindedness and rigidity. This characteristic has significant consequences for management decision-making; it has been discovered that dogmatic managers make judgments rapidly, based on minimal information, and with a high degree of confidence in their conclusions' correctness. Dogmatism is described as the refusal to accept the beliefs, ideas, and behaviours of others. Individuals that are dogmatic have a hard time grasping new concepts. They are unable to accept sensible ideas in place of their erroneous ones. They don't work well with those who have opposing viewpoints.

72.Analytical Behaviour

Analytical—this personality type is known for its ability to collect and analyze data. This is the type of person who works in technical fields like engineering, accountancy, and information technology. These people value precision and accuracy, and they take great delight in presenting accurate information. In order to test and validate the origin of the problem and design solutions to resolve the problems found, a person must be able to identify and define problems, extract critical information from data, and develop feasible solutions for the problems discovered.

73. Task Performance and Contextual Performance

The work activities that contribute to an organization's technological core are referred to as task performance. Task performance is more likely to be mandated by the official job function, whereas contextual performance is more likely to be voluntary. Employees' activities that contribute to an organization's social and psychological core are referred to as contextual performance. Work performance has traditionally been limited to the core task activities that are purely dependent on a job analysis (Campbell 1990; Jex & Britt 2008).

However, contextual performance, which refers to discretionary behaviours relating to the support of other employees in the company, has recently been added to the idea (Becker & Kernan 2006; Katz & Kahn1978). Because task performance is concerned with behaviours required to complete job tasks, while contextual performance is required to safeguard and upgrade the organization's organizational, social, and psychological environment, both aspects of job performance are critical to achieving organizational objectives.

74. Organizational Citizenship Behaviour

Individual, discretionary activities taken by employees outside of their formal job description are referred to as organizational citizenship behaviours (OCBs). Dennis Organ and his colleagues (cf. Bateman & Organ, 1983; Smith, Organ, & Near, 1983) initially established the phrase "Organizational Citizenship Behaviour" over a decade and a half ago (OCBs). Organ (1988: 4) defined organizational citizenship behaviours as "individual behaviour that is discretionary, not directly or explicitly recognized by the formal reward system, and that in the aggregate promotes the effective functioning of the organization," drawing on Chester Barnard's (Barnard, 1938) concept of "willingness to cooperate" and Daniel Katz's (Katz, 1964; Katz & Kahn, 1966, 1978) distinction between dependable role performance and "innovative and spontaneous behaviours."

By discretionary, it means that the behaviour is not an enforceable requirement of the role or job description, i.e., the clearly specified terms of the person's employment contract with the organization; rather, the behaviour is a matter of personal choice, and its omission is not generally understood as punishable.

75. Counterproductive Work Behaviours.

Employee voluntary behaviours that damage organizations are denoted as (CWB-O), or persons working in organizations are referred to as counterproductive work behaviour (CWB) (CWB-P). Destruction of business property, calling in sick while not unwell, criticizing another employee, and stealing from the employer are all examples of CWB's actions. OCB was first defined by two criteria (Bateman & Organ, 1983; Smith, Organ, & Near, 1983) in the early study (Bateman & Organ, 1983; Smith, Organ, & Near, 1983). (1) Organizationally functional behaviour that goes above and beyond role requirements.

Organ (1988), citing Graham, later included "civic virtue" as a type of OCB in his book on the subject but kept the general OCB construct as organizationally useful, extra-role conduct. Employee actions that are harmful to both individuals and organizations are classified as counterproductive workplace habits (CWBs; Fox & Spector, 2004). "CWB is regarded as an umbrella term that subsumes, in part or whole, similar ideas involving harmful behaviours at work," Spec- tor and Fox (2010) added (p. 133). Aggression, deviance, retribution, and revenge are all examples of CWB behaviours.

76.Joining and Staying With the Organization

Another crucial activity that has grown increasingly important to firms around the world is joining and remaining with the organization. Even with a larger pool to choose from due to the weak economy, finding appropriate people for certain job groups remains difficult. Even if they do find the ideal individual for the position, retaining that employee overtime is a daily problem for businesses. It is more expensive to replace staff than to keep them. From the top-down, it is vital for firms to build a join and stay culture.

77.Maintaining Work Attendance

All firms rely on their employees to arrive at work on time. For employers, poor attendance is a constant source of anxiety (Organization Behaviour, 2016). Employees in the United States miss an average of only five days per year from scheduled work, but even this low level of absenteeism can disrupt the workflow of other employees and damage customer service (Organization Behaviour, 2016).

Presenteeism

According to Aronsson, Gustafsson and Dallner (2000), presenteeism refers to 'the phenomenon of people, who despite complaints and ill health that should prompt rest and absence from work, are still turning up at their jobs' (p. 503).

In much of the existing research, presenteeism is viewed not as a habit but as the costs it entails in terms of lost output. Presenteeism, for example, is defined by the American College of Occupational and Environmental Medicine as 'the measurable extent to which health symptoms, conditions and diseases adversely affect the productivity of individuals who choose to remain at work when ill' (Chapman, 2005, p. 2). Absenteeism is often regarded as a behaviour, and it is theoretically more consistent to consider both absenteeism and presenteeism activities that result in costly repercussions. The behavioural definition of presenteeism is employed here to refer to persons who work through illness in order to be consistent with absenteeism research. Employees who are absent without cause are said to be absenteeism, whilst employees who are present but not working are said to be presenteeism.

Sickness Presenteeism is a relatively new idea, and several researchers have suggested that it can be defined in two ways. Sickness presenteeism is defined as "those who, despite complaints and ill health that should compel rest and absence from work, continue to show up to their jobs." The other meaning, known as 'impaired work function,' is "a diminished performance at work, other than disease." Sickness presenteeism has become a more prevalent topic in recent years. Cary Cooper invented the word in the 1990s to characterize a growing trend among workers who worked long hours because they were afraid of losing their jobs (Chapman, 2005).

78. Workplace Gossiping

Workplace gossip is a type of informal communication among coworkers that focuses on other people's private, personal, and sensitive matters. Negative workplace gossip causes social undermining and has significant negative consequences for employees. Negative gossip, on the other hand, causes the most harm to the employee who believes he or she is being singled out. Gossip is a powerful technique for strengthening informal employee relationships in firms (Noon and Delbridge, 1993; Dunbar, 2004; Kniffin and Wilson, 2005). Negative workplace gossip is defined as "negative, informal, and evaluative conversation in an organization about another member of that organization who is not there" (de Gouveia et al., 2005; Chandra and Robinson, 2010; Wu et al., 2016).

Negative workplace gossip can have serious consequences for employees (Baumeister and Leary, 1995; Ellwardt et al., 2012), such as lowering work efficiency and job satisfaction (Michelson and Mouly, 2000; Greengard, 2001) and causing more harm than good to their team (Elias and Scotson, 1994). It shatters togetherness, makes everyone uneasy, and erodes mutual trust, all of which have a negative impact on workers' work attitudes and conduct (Aquino and Thau, 2009; Chandra and Robinson, 2010).

79. Workplace Incivility

Cyber incivility is a type of electronic aggressiveness that occurs in the workplace, specifically through the use of emails (Lim & Teo, 2009). When it comes to studying, cyberbullying is a subgroup of cyber harassment that has been connected primarily to youth (Willard, 2011). Low-intensity deviant behaviour with uncertain intent to hurt the target has been classified as workplace incivility. Incivility behaviour is characterized by rudeness and discourteousness, as well as a lack of consideration for others. Low-intensity deviant behaviour with uncertain intent to hurt the target is classified as workplace incivility (Andersson and Pearson, 1999).

Uncivil behaviour is a stressor that might have poor health effects (e.g., depression and physical symptoms; Jex et al., 1992; Spector and Jex, 1998). Interpersonal abuse can be harmful to one's self-esteem on a psychological level (i.e., offence to self; Cornish-Bowden, 2004). Incivility can lower a person's self-esteem (Frone, 2000), self-efficacy (Mikkelsen and Einarsen, 2002), self-confidence (Vartia, 2001), and well-being (Lapierre et al., 2005). Incivility appears to be negatively connected with job satisfaction, psychological well-being, and life satisfaction, according to empirical studies. Furthermore, it is linked to increased levels of occupational stress, job withdrawal, and psychological suffering (Lim and Cortina, 2005).

80. Workplace Bullying

Workplace bullying is defined as a pattern of mistreatment by coworkers that results in physical or emotional harm. Verbal, nonverbal, psychological, and physical abuse, as well as humiliation, can all be used. There is no single definition for bullying, particularly workplace bullying, in the literature. According to Namie (2003), bullying can be seen as a continuum that begins with incivility, progresses to bullying, and finally culminates in workplace violence. Martucci and Sinatra (2009) claimed that there are no particular federal statutes that ban workplace bullying, in addition to the inconsistent definitions in a wide body of literature.

Negative deeds, undesirable, source of power, a target having difficulties defending oneself, and having the aim to damage the target are some of the important terms that occurred in definitions in the literature. There is a lot of room for a variety of subtle approaches in the job, and the parameters are wide. Bullying behaviours can be classified into the following categories: threats to professional status (e.g. belittling opinions, public, professional humiliation, accusations of lack of effort); threats to personal standing (e.g. name-calling, insults, intimidation, devaluing with regard to age); isolation (e.g. preventing access to opportunities, physical or social isolation, withholding of information); overwork (e.g. undue pressure, impossible deadlines, unnecessary disruptions); and destabilization (e.g. failure to give credit when due, meaningless tasks, removal of responsibility, repeated reminders of blunders, setting up to fail).

81. Workplace Insolence

Workplace An employee's insolence is derogatory, scornful, or abusive language or actions directed at the employer, which may be communicated in a confrontational manner. An employee's willful unwillingness to accept the employer's legitimate and reasonable directions is known as insubordination. Acts or actions that are excessively disrespectful to a boss and potentially verbally abusive are classified as insolence. Yelling at supervisors or coworkers, refusing to comply with a supervisor's legitimate request, negatively impacting others' work, or destroying client interactions or company growth dealings are all examples of insolence. Harassing behaviour, bragging about non-compliance, and questioning the status quo in a way that is detrimental to the organization are all examples. Insolence is not a professional argument; instead, it is a heated private chat that passes quickly.

82. Exhibiting Insubordination

In the workplace, insubordination refers to an employee's willful failure to follow an employer's lawful and reasonable demands. A supervisor's level of respect and ability to supervise would be harmed by such a rejection, which is frequently grounds for disciplinary action, up to and including termination. Insubordination is a form of disobedience that displays belligerent defiance of authority. Insubordination is defined as a purposeful violation of supervisory authority, which indicates that the employee is ultimately responsible.

83. Humility

In the workplace, humility entails being open to constructive criticism and feedback, as well as exhibiting respect and acknowledging others' roles and contributions. Employee job happiness is also aided by a humble work environment. Employees can feel empowered and validated when their leaders demonstrate humility by asking for their perspectives, adopting ideas for how to better serve customers and clients, and recognizing team members who have made a difference. Humble leadership is defined as a leadership style in which a leader views himself and his subordinates through a holistic and objective lens, valuing the positive worth, strengths, and contributions of his or her subordinates (Owens et al., 2013; Yuan et al., 2018).

It has three behavioural components: (a) accepting one's limitations and mistakes; (b) highlighting employees' contributions and strengths; and (c) remaining open to guidance, ideas, and feedback (Owens et al., 2013; Owens and Hekman, 2016). According to SIP theory, modest leadership embodies significant and useful social information that can be used to shape employees' views and affect their reactions through the use of language and symbols.

Furthermore, modest leadership promotes supportive organizational environments, such as an empowering climate (Ou et al., 2014), legitimization of subordinate growth and development (Owens and Hekman, 2012), and employee learning reinforcement. It is strongly related to the concept of resilience, which, as previously said, stresses good coping and progress. Furthermore, modest leadership facilitates communication (Elrod, 2013), enhances psychological safety (Walters and Diab, 2016), and fosters organizational trust (Elrod, 2013; Cooper et al., 2019), all of which are critical antecedents to employee resilience (Cooper et al., 2019).

84. Perceived insider identity /Status

Perceived insider identity refers to "the extent to which an individual employee perceives him or herself as an insider within a particular organization" (Stamper and Masterson, 2002, p. 876; also see Schaubroeck et al., 2017). It provides a "reason to" type of motivation that encourages proactive employee reactions (Schaubroeck et al., 2017; Parker et al., 2010, p. 830). perceived insider status (PIS) among employees, with PIS being defined as "the extent to which an individual employee perceives himself or herself as an insider within a particular organization" (Stamper and Masterson, 2002, p. 876). It signifies that employees have earned "personal space" and acceptability inside their workplace. According to research, PIS has a significant impact on employee work performance and organizational citizenship behaviour (OCB), among other things. Individuals identify themselves and others into social groups according to social identity theory (Tajfel, 1982) and social categorization theory (Turner, 1987).

85. Adaptability

Adaptability in the workplace refers to the ability to alter and be flexible in order to succeed. When selecting applicants, businesses look for adaptability as a soft skill. Employees in leadership positions are frequently faced with unique situations for which there are no precise instructions. According to Hall (2002), adaptability is a career meta competency that, along with personal identity, constitutes the core of a protean career. It is, at its essence, the ability to change, which includes both the ability and the desire to do so (Hall & Chandler, 2005). However, recent research has focused on adaptive behaviour in relation to certain job types (Pulakos et al., 2000). Adaptability has been defined as "the capacity of actors in a system to influence resilience" (Walker et al. 2004:5).

*Transformability has been defined as "the capacity to create a fundamentally new system when ecological, economic, or social structures make the existing system untenable" (Walker et al. 2004:5). Transformability means "capable of being changed".

86. Teamwork Behaviour/ Cohesive Team

Team-building behaviour refers to the activities or efforts that help a group connect with one another. The "after the fact" effect of team building is team cohesion. To keep the team-building activities going, team cohesion must be maintained. In the workplace, teamwork refers to when a group of people works together to achieve a common goal in a timely and effective manner. Your business can thrive when different people work together toward a single goal. Make sure you learn to connect with your teammates when studying collaboration behaviours.

This entails being able to understand what other people are going through. Other elements of a project may not be doing well, and you must be able to grasp what other team members are going through.

Not only are group goals attained when a team is cohesive, but everyone feels like they contributed to the group's overall success. Individuals on a cohesive team are more driven to work toward the team goal and focus on the complete group rather than their own selves. If each of the five characteristics defined by Lencioni is maximized, a team will work as efficiently and effectively as feasible. Trust, Conflict, Commitment, Accountability, and Results are the traits of a cohesive team. Each behaviour in the model builds on the one before it and helps to sustain the others.

87.Problem-Solving Ability

A person's capacity to successfully handle and discover answers for complicated and unexpected situations is referred to as problem-solving. Candidates with strong problem-solving abilities are able to think analytically as well as creatively. Problem-solving skills allow you to figure out why something is happening and how to fix it. It's one of the most important abilities that businesses look for in job candidates. Identifying the problem, developing solutions, executing those solutions, and assessing their efficacy are all steps in the problem-solving process.

88.Confidence

Confidence is a clear-headed belief in the correctness of a theory or forecast or in the best or most effective course of action. Confidence is derived from the Latin word 'fire,' which means "to trust," therefore, self-confidence is trust in oneself. Your belief or faith in anything is referred to as confidence. It can refer to your confidence in your ability to do your job and in yourself in the workplace. This mindset implies that you are aware of your own abilities, expertise, and ultimate capabilities. Self-confidence is a mindset about one's own strengths and skills.

It implies that you accept and trust yourself and that you are in command of your life. You have a good outlook on yourself and are aware of your talents and weaknesses. You speak assertively, set realistic expectations and goals, and can handle criticism.

89. Dependability

Being dependable entails doing what you say you'll do when you say you'll do it. You can be counted on to perform any work with excellence. A dependable person establishes trust by holding themselves and, if he or she leads others, their subordinates are accountable. Dependable when it comes to completing job-related activities, completing assigned assignments, and keeping deadlines and appointments. Because there is a high level of trust among the team, employers may focus on more vital duties such as growth and development.

90. Working independently

Working independently refers to the ability to complete activities on one's own. A supervisor or manager may give you project direction, but they can then trust you to do duties with little to no oversight. What does it imply to be self-sufficient? It entails becoming self-aware, self-monitoring, and self-correcting, knowing what you need to do rather than waiting to be told what to do, and taking the initiative rather than waiting to be told what to do. Doing what is required of you to the best of your ability, without external nudging, and working until the job is finished. Learning to work at a pace that you can keep up with is essential. Take responsibility for your mistakes rather than looking for excuses; and refusing to get carried away by self-doubt or bad emotions triggered by unfavourable prior experiences. Self-awareness, self-motivation, and self-regulation are essential for independence.

91. Workplace Harassment

Harassment in the workplace refers to insulting or threatening behaviour directed against a single employee or a group of employees. Workplace harassment is defined as "any unfavourable workplace interpersonal interaction that has an impact on an individual's job terms, conditions, or employment decisions, or produces an intimidating, hostile, or offensive working environment, but is based on any legally unprotected characteristic" (Rospenda & Richman, 2004, p. 221 222). Workplace bullying (Einarsen, Hoel, Zapf, & Cooper, 2011), incivility (Cortina, Magley, Williams, & Langhout, 20 01), victimization (Aquino & Lamertz, 2004), social undermining (Duffy, Gangster, & Pagon, 20 02), and abusive supervision have all been investigated as forms of harassment (Tepper, 2000).

92. Workplace Victimization

Victimization at work is an act of aggression committed by one employee or a group of employees against another employee with the intent of harming the victim. Harm to the victim can include long-term physical, psychological, or emotional harm. When an employee's well-being is jeopardized at work as a result of an act of hostility perpetrated by one or more members of the company, this is known as workplace victimization. Among the ones frequently appearing in the literature on aggressive behaviour are "workplace harassment" (Bjorkqvist et al. 1994, Bowling & ¨ Beehr 2006), "mobbing" (Leymann 1996, Zapf et al. 1996), "petty tyranny" (Ashforth 1997), "bullying" (e.g., Einarsen & Skogstad 1996, Salin 2003b, Vartia 1996), "emotional abuse" (Keashly 1998), "abusive supervision" (Tepper 2000), "social undermining" (Duffy et al. 2002), "incivility" (Andersson & Pearson 1999, Cortina et al. 2001), "identity threats" (Aquino & Douglas 2003), and "victimisation" (Aquino et al. 1999). Victimisation at work is an act of aggression committed by one employee or a group of employees against another employee with the intent of harming the victim. Harm to the victim can include long-term physical, psychological, or emotional harm. Victimisation in the workplace encompasses a wide variety of deviant behaviour. Physical attacks, bullying, harassment, racial bigotry, sexual harassment, malicious gossip, and undermining a person's authority are all manifestations of workplace victimisation. As a result, workplace victimisation can include both physical and mental abuse.

93. Social Undermining

According to Duffy, Ganster, and Pagon (2002), social undermining in the workplace is defined as behaviour that is meant to undermine a person's ability to create or maintain strong interpersonal relationships over time. The expressing of negative feelings or unfavourable assessments directed towards a specific person as a means of preventing that person from accomplishing their goals is known as social undermining. This action is frequently linked to negative emotions like hate or rage. "Behaviour intended to impede, over time, the ability to build and maintain positive interpersonal relationships, work-related achievement, and favourable reputation" is how social undermining is defined (Duffy et al., 2002: p. 332).

94. Workplace Absenteeism

Absenteeism is described as an employee's absence from work for a period of time that exceeds what is considered acceptable. Absenteeism has long been seen as significant human resource management (HRM) issue in a variety of industries and organizations (Bycio, 1992; Harrison and Martocchio, 1998). A significant body of economic literature is devoted to absenteeism, examining the influence of a wide range of variables on worker behaviour (see, among others, Dionne and Dostie, 2007; Barmby, Ercolani, and Treble, 2002). Some of these variables are linked to personal traits (gender, age, education, health status, and so on), while others are linked to contractual and institutional factors (such as the generosity of sickness benefits, the degree of employment protection, firm size, type of job, labour market conditions, etc.). Absenteeism is defined as "a regular absence from work for one or more days, frequently excused by a medical certificate but, in reality, due to personal interests and a lack of sense of responsibility."

95.Machiavellianism / Machiavellian Personality

A word used to characterize a company's political manoeuvring. Used to describe someone who is a master manipulator and abuser of authority. Machiavellianism is a psychological trait that signifies cunning, manipulative ability, and a desire to obtain power by any means necessary. Along with narcissism and psychopathy, Machiavellianism is one of the qualities that make up the Dark Triad. Machiavellianism is a notion that is gaining in popularity, particularly in the field of personality studies (Rauthmann, 2012). People with high levels of Machiavellianism (Christie and Geis, 1970) are characterized by interpersonal manipulation, such as flattery and deception, as well as aloof, cynical, and conventionally amoral perspectives adopted to further their own goals/interests (Christie and Geis, 1970; Fehr et al., 1992; McHoskey, 1995; McHoskey et al., 1998; Wilson et al., 1998; Bereczkei et al., 2010). People who are Machiavellian behave in a self-interested manner, manipulating others for personal gain (Gunnthorsdottir, McCabe, & Smith, 2002; Wilson, Near, & Miller, 1996). Individuals with high Mach scores (also known as "high Mach individuals") show a proclivity to be callous, greedy, and nasty in their interpersonal interactions (Paulhus & Williams, 2002). In each situation, they choose the appropriate strategy coolly and sensibly, and they do not make emotional decisions (Jones & Paulhus, 2009). Low Machs are on the other end of the Mach range and are known for being extremely docile. Individuals with a low Mach orientation are willing to follow instructions and flourish in highly organized environments.

96.Masculinity-Femininity

In society, high masculinity means boldness, domination, and independence. In a culture, high femininity denotes dependency, compassion, and emotional opinions. Machiavellianism refers to a person who has a bad reputation for interacting with people to achieve his or her own goals and for manipulating others for his or her own gain (Christie and Geis, 1970, p. 1). An individual's general approach to interacting with other people, as well as the degree to which they believe they may control others in interpersonal circumstances, is known as a Machiavellian attitude (Robinson and Shaver, 1973, p. 590). To achieve personal or organizational goals, a modern-day Machiavellian uses aggressive, manipulative, exploitative, and deceptive tactics (Calhoon, 1969, p. 211). Others in the organization's needs, feelings, and rights are secondary. We define "traditional masculinity" and "traditional femininity" as long-lasting characteristics that include attributes, appearances, interests, and behaviours that have traditionally been associated with men and women, respectively (adapting the definitions provided by Constantinople, 1973). Deaux and Lewis (1984) explored the perceived relationship between gender and gender-related components, such as role behaviours (e.g., head of household vs takes care of children), features, jobs, and physical attributes, in a seminal study on masculinity and femininity (e.g., tall, broad-shouldered vs soft voice, graceful). The researchers discovered that these elements were interrelated, influencing one another as well as gender and sexual orientation perceptions.

97.Skunkworks

A small group of engineers, technicians, and/or designers are assigned to a specialized team and segregated from the rest of the company; the team's purpose is to generate novel ideas, products, or services as quickly as possible. A SkunkWorks project (also known as Skunk Works) is an innovative endeavour involving a small group of people that takes place outside of an organization's standard research and development channels. The term "skunkworks" or "skunkworks" is commonly used in business, engineering, and technology sectors to denote a group inside an organization that is given a high degree of autonomy and is free of bureaucracy and is tasked with working on advanced or secret projects.

98.Social Learning

In natural resource management, social learning is increasingly becoming a normative objective (e.g., Parson and Clark 1995, Diduck et al. 2005, Keen et al. 2005a, Reed et al., 2006). Albert Bandura, a noted psychologist, launched a continuation of Skinner's study. Bandura considers behaviour to be the result of constant interaction between cognitive (person), behavioural, and environmental factors. Bandura, unlike Skinner, argues that cognitive functioning should not be overlooked when understanding and changing behaviour. Employers can take advantage of this by encouraging social learning among their personnel. The collection and sharing of information gained through peers and social media are referred to as social learning. It's also possible that this is how a rapidly expanding part of the workforce chooses to study. Ison and Watson (2007) define social learning "as achieving concerted action in complex and uncertain situations."

99. Pro-environmental Behaviour

The terms "social learning" and "environmental behaviour" are commonly used interchangeably and defined as "behaviour that has a reduced impact on the environment (including, for example, switching off lights, recycling and using sustainable modes of travel)" (Reid et al., in press). For example, Pahl-Wostl et al. (2008) call social learning "sustainable learning" that consists of "developing new identities, as well as institutions and individual capacities, that are more socially and ecologically robust with the common goal of sustainability". This is echoed by Tàbara and Pahl-Wostl (2007), who assert that "the notion of sustainability as a social learning process is now pervasive..."

100. Employee Green Behaviour

Employees' green behaviour refers to a series of behaviours implemented by employees that aim at reducing the negative effect on the environment and contributing to environmental sustainability.

Pro-environmental or green behaviour is behaviour that minimises harm to the environment as much as possible or even benefits it (Steg & Vlek, 2009). Examples include minimising energy use and reducing waste. More simply, it has been described as 'doing good and avoiding bad' (Cushman-Roisin, 2012).

101. Social support

Individual or group comfort, aid, or information gained through official or informal relationships. "Support accessible to an individual through social relationships to other individuals, groups, and the greater community" is how social support is defined. The sense or experience that one is loved and cared for by others, revered and cherished and part of a social network of mutual help and obligations is defined as social support (Wills, 1991). A partner, relatives, friends, workplace, social and community ties, and even a beloved pet can provide social support (Allen, Blascovich, & Mendes, 2002). Support has typically been categorized into numerous distinct categories in taxonomies of social support.

When one person assists another in better understanding a distressing incident and determining what resources and coping methods may be required to deal with it, this is known as informational assistance. A person under stress can use this knowledge or counsel to identify exactly what costs or stresses the stressful event may entail and how to effectively handle them. Instrumental support entails the provision of concrete aid in the form of services, financial aid, and other specialized aid or items. Driving an injured buddy to the emergency room or feeding a bereaved family are two examples.

*Emotional support entails giving another person warmth and nurturing, as well as telling them that they are a valuable person for whom people care. However, as the term indicates, social support can also refer to the belief that such resources are available in the event that they are required.

102. Stereotype

A stereotype is a fixed, overgeneralized belief about a certain group or class of people in social psychology. Stereotyping implies that a person possesses a set of features and talents that we presume are shared by all members of that group (McLeod, 2017). A self-perpetuating assumption about people's personal attributes that are overgeneralized, oversimplified, and oversimplified.

* When you're in a scenario where you're afraid of unwittingly confirming a negative stereotype, you're dealing with a stereotype threat. The mere realization that a negative group stereotype can apply to you in a specific situation triggers it.

Even if the person does not believe the stereotype, the person may feel threatened. Steele claims that stereotype threat induces "spotlight anxiety" (Steele & Aronson, 1995, p. 809), which leads to mental distress and "vigilant worry," which can lead to performance problems.

103. Creativity

The ability of a person to come up with fresh ideas or new perspectives on old ones. Both academics and practitioners frequently use the terms "creativity" and "innovation" interchangeably (Scott and Bruce, 1994). Despite their similarities, these frameworks have unique emphases. The term "creativity" has been defined in a variety of ways in the literature. The production of fresh or original ideas that are valuable is a common thread for the majority of them. For example, Amabile (1983) and Mumford and Gustafson (1988) define creativity as the development of new and useful ideas. Furthermore, when scholars use the term "creativity," they frequently allude to something that has never been done before (Woodman et al., 1993). Employees who have the flexibility and option of how to complete a task work more innovatively, according to researchers (Amabile & Gitomer, 1984; Sun, Zhang, Qi, & Chen, 2012).

104.   Cultural values

Cultural values are the fundamental concepts and ideas that underpin a community's existence, protection, and reliance on harmonious relationships. Employee values must be held and acted upon in order for the organization to act on strategic ideals.

Culture is defined as "the human-made part of the environment (Herskovits, 1955). It has both objective elements- tools, roads, appliances- and subjective elements- categories, associations, beliefs, attitudes, norms, roles, and values" (Triandis, 1994: p. 113). Workplace attitudes and actions are shaped by cultural beliefs (Triandis, 1994). Culture also shapes the area of normative conduct (e.g., behaviour that is desired for members of the culture vs behaviour that is condemned), establishes roles for individuals in the social structure, and prescribes guiding principles and values in one's life. As a result, culture dictates how items in the environment, such as an organization's practices, rules, and procedures, are appraised, as well as how people react to those processes (Robert et al., 2000). Compensation schemes reflect these cultural beliefs. Performance and knowledge, which reflect equity, are the most common pay basis in the United States (Heneman and Werner, 2005).

According to this international research, there are three main principles that determine compensation award decisions for individuals: fairness, equality, and need. Individuals should be compensated based on their contributions, such as task performance, according to the equity rule. Individuals should be compensated equally regardless of their contributions to the group or organization, according to the equality rule. Individuals should be paid based on their own needs, according to the need rule.

I.   *The Hofstede Dimensions*
Hofstede (1994, p. 5) defined his value dimensions thus:

Power distance is "the degree of inequality which the population of a country considers as normal." Uncertainty avoidance is "the degree to which people in a country prefer structured over unstructured situations."

Individualism is "the degree to which people in a country prefer to act as individuals rather than as members of groups."

Masculinity/femininity is "the degree to which values like assertiveness, performance, success and competition, which is nearly all societies is associated with the role of men, prevails over values like the quality of life, maintaining warm personal relationships, service, care for the weak and solidarity, which is nearly all societies are more associated with the role of women."

### II.	*The Schwartz Culture-Level Dimensions*

Schwartz (1994, 1999) polled 60,000 people in 63 countries about their value preferences. Secondary school instructors and students were offered as samples in several nations. Individual-level and country-level data analyses were carried out separately. He selected seven country-level value orientations that are relevant to apply in the current culture-level investigation.

Conservatism, or embeddedness (as the latter word is used in this article), stresses the preservation of the status quo, appropriateness, and restraint of acts or tendencies that can disturb the solidary group or the established order in which people are embedded. "Intellectual autonomy emphasizes the desirability of individuals pursuing their own ideas and intellectual directions independently". Affective autonomy emphasizes the desirability of individuals' to pursue affectively positive experiences. "Hierarchy" stresses the validity of uneven power, positions, and resource distribution. Egalitarianism stresses the transcending of one's own self-interests in favour of a voluntary commitment to the betterment of others. "Mastery" promotes active self-assertion as a means of going ahead. Harmony highlights the importance of blending in with the surroundings.

## 105.	Defensive avoidance

Because there appears to be little possibility of finding a better solution, it entails making no modifications to current activities and avoiding any future engagement with related concerns. The decision makers' attempt to avoid or postpone the stress of choice is known as defensive avoidance. Procrastination, shifting of duty, and rationalization are all signs of it. Individuals who either reject the seriousness of a risk or an opportunity or deny any responsibility for taking action have a condition that prevents them from making successful decisions.

106. Extinction Behaviour

Extinction is defined as the cessation of a taught habit. You can put an end to behaviour by depriving it of the positive reward that prompted it in the first place. As an example, assume you have an employee who is always interfering with the work of your other team members. Reduces the frequency of conduct by removing a reward or desired result associated with it. Extinction is a behavioural word that involves determining the function/cause of a behaviour and then terminating access to that function to extinguish the behaviour. You figure out what the behaviour's reinforcement is, and then you don't give it to them. There are several varieties of extinction, including * Tangible Extinction (when a person is denied access to a wanted thing or activity) and * Escape Extinction (when a person is denied access to a desired item or activity) (the person does not get to avoid or escape a non-preferred task or person).

107. Gatekeeping Theory

Kurt Zadek Lewin was born in Germany in 1890 and died in 1947. He was a brilliant Psychologist and a forerunner in the field of Social

Psychology. In order to comprehend human behaviour and the importance of whole living space, he invented the notion of psychological "field" and "living space" in the area of psychology. His research focuses on gaining a better understanding of a person's physical, mental, and social worlds by having regular conversations with his pre-memories, desires, and ambitions. His study also aids in the understanding of the link between group or individual attitudes and behaviour. "Gatekeeping" is a term coined by Kurt Lewin. It's nothing more than employing a fence to keep undesirable or unnecessary items out. The individual who makes a choice is referred to as the "Gatekeeper" in this case. It is widely utilized in the discipline of psychology at first and then in the field of communication subsequently. It is now considered one of the most important ideas in communication studies. The Gatekeeper determines whether information should be passed on to a group or individual and which should not. The gatekeepers are the decision-makers who allow the entire social system to function. The gatekeeper has its own social, cultural, ethical, and political effects. They disseminate knowledge to the group based on personal or societal factors.

A person who occupies a strategic location in the network and has the ability to manipulate information flowing in either way through a channel. The process of filtering material for dissemination, whether for printing, radio, the internet, or any other medium of communication, is known as gatekeeping (communication).

108.   Job Hopping

When a person makes fewer modifications inside a company and goes to new companies to develop his or her career, this occurs. The practice of holding many jobs in a short period of time is referred to as "job-hopping." It's usually characterized as a job that lasts fewer than two years. Frequent job changes, which were long considered a red flag on applications, have grown increasingly normal in today's workplace. Job unhappiness, health difficulties, or a desire for a career shift are all reasons to consider changing employment. Job hopping is annoying for some people, but it is crucial for others. Due to COVID-19, your job may have been terminated or your responsibilities modified. Others, on the other hand, intentionally employ job-hopping to locate their ideal career.

109.   Conflict at Workplace

Conflict is an inevitable aspect of every job, yet it may lead to absenteeism, lost productivity, and mental health difficulties. Conflict, on the other hand, maybe a motivation for new ideas and creativity, as well as enhanced flexibility and a better understanding of working relationships. Conflict, on the other hand, must be skillfully managed in order for organizations to succeed.

110.   Conflict Management Styles

Five Major Conflict Management Styles

Knowing when and how to employ each style may assist manage conflict and creating a better working environment, all of which contribute to a higher bottom line.

I. *Collaborative Style:*

Combining assertiveness with cooperation, collaborators seek to work with others to find a solution that truly addresses everyone's concerns. This method, which is the polar opposite of avoidance, allows both parties to obtain what they want while minimizing bad sentiments. "Collaboration works best when the long-term relationship and outcome are crucial," Dr Benoliel explains. "For example, preparing to merge two departments into one, where you want the best of both in the newly created department."

II. *Competing Style:*

Competitors are outspoken and uncooperative, and they are eager to pursue their own objectives at the expense of others. Dr Benoliel adds that this technique is effective when the connection is unimportant, but the outcome is critical, such as when competing for a new customer with another firm. "Do not utilize competition within your business; it does not foster connections," she warns.

III. *Avoiding Confrontation Style:*

When diplomatically sidestepping an issue or just withdrawing from a frightening circumstance, those who avoid conflict tend to be unassertive and disagreeable. "Use this when it's safer to put off dealing with an issue, or you don't care as much about the outcome, such as if you're having a disagreement with a coworker overusing FaceTime at work."

IV. *Accommodating Style:*

When adapting to satisfy the other person, there is an element of self-sacrifice, which is the polar opposite of competing. While it may appear to be generous, it may be exploiting the vulnerable and causing animosity. "You may utilize accommodating when you don't care about the outcome but want to maintain or strengthen the connection," Dr Benoliel explains. "For example, going out to lunch with the boss and agreeing, 'If you want to go for Thai food for lunch, that's OK with me.'"

V.   Compromising Style:

This approach seeks to create a quick, mutually acceptable solution that partially satisfies both sides while preserving assertiveness and cooperation. "This method is excellent to utilize when the conclusion is not critical, and you are wasting time," Dr Benoliel explains. "For example, when you just want to make a choice and move on to more important things and are prepared to sacrifice a bit to get the decision made." "However, be aware that no one is truly content," she says.

111.   Blocking role.

A role that focuses on stopping the group from attaining its objective. It refers to a group member's activities that are centred on his or her personal well-being, frequently at the expense of other members of the group, obstructing the group's ability to achieve its purpose. Activities that disturb the group are known as blocking roles. They may dominate talks, verbally attack other members of the group, or distract the group with irrelevant material or inappropriate comedy. It's possible that the blocking behaviour isn't meant to be bad.

112. Bluffing

Bluffing, or what some refer to as "mutual deception," is one of the most prevalent infractions of truthtelling in the workplace. Bluffing can be legal if both parties realize that the truth isn't always anticipated and the bluffing is seen as part of the bargaining process. A method used by negotiators. It is an act of deception in which you deceive the other person into believing that you will do something when you do not intend to do so. They try to persuade others to agree with them by making deliberate misstatements, concealing relevant information, or exaggerating—in other words, through bluffing. Albert Carr, writing in the Harvard Business Review in 1968, may have written the most famous justification of bluffing in business. This is an element of the caveat emptor ("buyer beware") ethic, which is compatible with Carr's notion of truthtelling. Carr went on to say that bluffing is an important part of savvy and efficient business strategy.

113. Boss-Centred Leadership Behaviour /Employee-Centred Leadership Behaviour

A more authoritarian boss who exhibits leadership behaviour on the Tannenbaum and Schmidt Leadership Continuum to the left. On the left is boss-centred leadership, while on the right is subordinate-centred leadership. Each behaviour point on the continuum represents the amount of decision-making power possessed by the boss and the employee, with each behaviour point reflecting the amount of decision-making authority possessed by the boss and the employee. On the left is boss-centred leadership, while on the right is subordinate-centred leadership. Each behaviour point on the continuum represents the amount of decision-making power possessed by the boss and the employee, with each behaviour point reflecting the amount of decision-making authority possessed by the boss and the employee.

* When a leader is engaged in building a cohesive workgroup and ensuring that employees are content with their tasks, this is referred to as "employee-centric leader conduct." These two leadership styles are seen to be at opposite extremes of the same continuum (Tannenbaum and Schmidt 1958).

Through the leader's self-realization and self-projection, "leader-centred styles" generate organizational success. Organizations that rely on authority, explicit orders, and rigorous deadlines are more likely to employ these techniques. They work in the way that the leader intends (Tannenbaum and Schmidt 1958).

* The situational leadership theory refers to leaders who use various leadership styles depending on the scenario and the development level of their team members. It's a good technique to lead since it adjusts to the demands of the team and strikes a good balance for the entire business.

114. Cognitive Intelligence

The general reasoning capacity refers to a systematic procedure of arriving at a certain conclusion by carefully considering all accessible or supplied information. Nonverbal reasoning, verbal reasoning, numerical reasoning, analytical reasoning, logical diagrams reasoning, symbolic reasoning, inductive reasoning, deductive reasoning, and abstract reasoning are all examples of mental talents. Human mental aptitude and understanding produced via thinking, experiences, and senses are referred to as cognitive intelligence. It's the ability to create new knowledge from existing data. Other cognitive skills such as attention, learning, memory, judgment, and reasoning are also included.

Human mental aptitude and understanding produced via thinking, experiences, and senses are referred to as cognitive intelligence. It's the ability to create new knowledge from existing data. Other cognitive skills such as attention, learning, memory, judgment, and reasoning are also included.

115. Democratic style

A leadership style in which the leader prioritizes both thoughtfulness and structure-building (in the Ohio State University studies). The term "democracy" refers to a government that is "governed by the people." Allowing different individuals to participate in the decision-making process is a hallmark of this leadership style. Participative leadership is a term used to describe democratic leadership. The democratic leader, according to Anderson (1959), is one who shares decision-making with the other members. In most instances, he claims, democratic leadership is related to improved morale. Democratic leadership is linked to greater productivity, contentment, participation, and commitment among followers (Hackman & Johnson, 1996). Democratic leadership, according to Chemers (1984), emphasizes collective engagement. As a result, democratic leadership is characterized by involvement (Bass, 1990). Knowledgeable, influential, stimulating, a winner of cooperation, a provider of logical consequences, encouraging, permitting self-determination, guiding, a good listener and respecting, and situation-centred are some of the characteristics of a democratic leader, according to Kuczmarski and Kuczmarski (1995). Distributing responsibilities among the membership, empowering group members, and assisting the group's decision-making process are all features of democratic leadership, according to Gastil (1994).

116. Ego state

One of the three behavioural patterns or psychological positions through which individuals connect with one another (parent, adult, and kid). In transactional analysis, ego states are not tied to a person's chronological age but are related to behavioural elements of age. 'Ego' does not have the same meaning in this situation as it does in our everyday lives (that is, self-importance). An Ego State is a state of being that a person is in at a certain time. Ego states are a recurring pattern of thought, emotion, and behaviour. Berne's tripartite model explains three major events that all of us go through: infancy, the formation of rational, logical thinking, and exposure to the influence of parents or important people.

* Ego-state therapy is a psychodynamic technique that uses parts to address a person's behavioural and cognitive issues. It employs group

and family therapy procedures, but with a solitary patient, to address problems that arise in a "family of self" within a single person.

117. Emotions and Emotional barriers

According to the American Psychological Association (APA), emotion is defined as "a complex reaction pattern, involving experiential, behavioural and physiological elements." Emotions are how people react to issues or circumstances that are important to them. A subjective experience, a physiological response, and a behavioural or expressive response are the three components of emotional experiences.

Individuals of diverse ages, classifications, and origins experience both happy and bad emotions throughout their life. Anger, frustration, tension, despair, anxiety, trauma, and pride are considered negative emotions, whereas happiness is considered a good emotion. Howard Weiss and Russell Cropanzano investigated the impact of six key emotions in the workplace: anger, fear, joy, love, sadness, and surprise (Weiss & Cropanzano, 1996). *An emotional barrier is a mental block that affects how you view others' behaviour and makes it difficult for you to express your thoughts accurately. Emotional barriers can cause an improper or ineffective emotional reaction. A common sort of communication obstacle. When the transmitter or recipient is emotional, obstructions might arise. They are severe disruptions triggered or exacerbated by feelings of wrath, fear, or hatred, among other things. Pride is an emotional barrier that affects how you see other people. It keeps you from focusing on anyone else's thoughts and ideas; save your own. For example, if you don't appreciate what the other person has to say, you're likely to dominate a conversation.

118. Emotional Intelligence

A form of human intelligence that allows a person to properly use his or her emotions. It is made up of a series of submental talents that let a person notice, analyze, and control emotions in himself and others. Emotional intelligence in the workplace begins with each individual from the inside out. It entails understanding different parts of your feelings and emotions, as well as devoting time to developing self-awareness, self-regulation, motivation, empathy, and social skills. Emotional intelligence has been identified as an essential notion in social psychology that is gradually becoming recognized. Emotional intelligence has recently received a lot of attention in the study, particularly in psychological research.

It is considered one of the most important aspects of both a successful life and psychological well-being (Bar-On, 2001). Emotional intelligence, according to Salovey et al. (1990), is the ability to hold emotional knowledge, recognize and manage emotions effectively, and encourage intellectual and emotional growth. Following that, the authors provided an updated and complete definition of emotional intelligence, which they defined as the capacity to detect feelings, coordinate feelings to inspire thinking, and comprehend and manage feelings to promote self-improvement (Mayer and Salovey, 1997).

Mayer et al. (1990) were well aware of their pivotal role in the development of emotional intelligence. Following that, in 1995, the development of the emotional intelligence concept began, with Daniel Goleman's work making a significant contribution.

119. Espoused Value

A value that is expressed as a value by the organization's employees. The degree to which individuals in the organization believe things should be is called espoused values. Individuals're the things they say are essential and meaningful to them. Shared Basic Assumptions are the deepest and most often secret level of ideas and values that are taken for granted and about which no one speaks. Espoused values are those that an organization or individual declares to believe in and want. Organizations' mission statements, presentations, taglines, and other materials frequently include espoused ideals. They are not intended to direct how employees in the company work but rather to motivate them to do so.

120. Entrepreneurial Leadership

A contemporary take on leadership. An entrepreneurial leader is one who possesses many of the qualities and actions of an entrepreneur. According to Babson College President Stephen Spinelli Jr., "Entrepreneurial leadership is a philosophy that focuses companies on converting issues into opportunities that produce economic and social value." Leadership is described as the process of influencing an organization's people in order to achieve organizational objectives (Esmer and Dayi, 2014, p.400). Leadership, on the other hand, is the capacity to inspire individuals to support and believe in the organization's aims (Dubrin, 2012, p.2). Despite the fact that there are several methods for defining leadership, research on leadership has grouped it into three categories: Great Man Theory, Traditional Leadership Theories, and New Leadership Theories. These theories are summarized by (Aksel, 2008, p.34).

121. Evaluation Apprehension

Nickolas B. Cottrell introduced the evaluation apprehension hypothesis in 1972. He said that we soon learn that the social rewards and punishments we receive are dependent on other people's assessments of us. In a conventional meeting, evaluation apprehension happens when a person has an excellent idea to give but is afraid to say anything. This fear could stem from a number of factors: the person may not feel comfortable speaking in public; the person may think the idea is good but isn't sure; or the person may not want to say something in front of his or her boss, who is also present, especially if the idea is critical of something the boss has done or is known to believe. As a result, the concept is never defined and hence may be lost forever.

122. Impression Management Behaviour

Impression management is a conscious or unconscious process in which people try to control and regulate information in social interactions in order to impact other people's views of a person, item, or event. Accounts (offering "explanations for a negative occurrence to avoid criticism"), excuses (denying "responsibility for poor outcomes"), and opinion conformity ("saying or behaving in ways congruent with the target") are only a few of the impressions management activities.

123. First-Impression Error

A perceptual mistake in which the perceiver forms a long-term impression of a person based on their first sight. It is human nature to judge a person based on a previous perception of that individual.

First impression error: This sort of prejudice permits your first impression of a candidate, whether positive or negative, to influence your input or choice. The majority of interview decisions are made during the first five seconds.

124. Irrational Behaviour

Individuals' irrational behaviours include taking offence or becoming angry over a situation that has not yet occurred, exaggerating emotions (such as crying hysterically), maintaining unrealistic expectations, and engaging in irresponsible behaviour such as problem intoxication, disorganization, and falling. Misinformation, emotional concerns, stress, and a hostile work environment are all major reasons for illogical conduct. Small business owners can engage with managers to address these core issues by advising treatment, proposing a transfer, or asking for their input on how the situation could be improved. The primary distinction between rational and irrational thinking is that rational thinking is founded on logic and reason, whereas irrational thinking is not.

When you say someone's sentiments and behaviour are illogical, you're implying that they're not founded on logic or clear reasoning.

125. Procrastinating Behaviour

Procrastination is defined as an unwelcome and unneeded delay, whether it is due to a lack of choice, implementation, or timeliness. (Lay, 1986; McCown et al., 1989; Mann et al., 1997; Steel, 2010). Furthermore, Steel (2007) noted that one of the essential characteristics of procrastination is the actor's understanding that the delay would make them worse off. As a result, procrastination might be viewed as illogical behaviour—delaying a planned course of action despite the fact that it is inconvenient (Klingsieck, 2013). There are at least two approaches to observing behavioural procrastination delay. First, during action execution, the individual may deviate to a more appealing option (Tice et al., 2001), causing the original plan to be delayed. Second, the detrimental repercussions of such distractions become obvious over time, such as when individuals postpone seeing their physicians until treatment is no longer an option (Worthley et al., 2006) or when people postpone starting their retirement plans (Byrne et al., 2006).

126. Good Cop, Bad Cop Routine

A distributive negotiating approach has two negotiators on your side, one who is polite and accommodating to the opposing party and the other who is tough and confrontational. Good cop/bad cop is a negotiation and interrogation psychological method in which two persons employ contrasting tactics to question their target Brodt and

Tuchinsky (2000). In order to persuade the subject to participate, one interrogator develops a harsh or accusatory tone, stressing threats of punishment, while the other adopts a more sympathetic approach, emphasizing rewards (Katie, 2020).

127. Pygmalion Effect

The Pygmalion effect, also known as the Rosenthal effect, is a psychological phenomenon in which high expectations result in better performance in a certain field. Mitchell and colleagues, 2003. Pygmalion, the sculptor who fell so much in love with the absolutely beautiful statue he sculpted that it came to life, is the inspiration for the effect. High expectations lead to higher performance, whereas low expectations lead to lower performance. According to Rosenthal and Jacobson and Mitchell et al., 2003, both effects contribute to a self-fulfilling prophecy. According to the Pygmalion effect, the targets of expectations internalize their positive labels, and those with positive labels prosper as a result; in the case of low expectations, a similar process operates in the reverse direction. The Pygmalion effect states that if the leader's expectation of the follower's performance is raised, the follower will perform better.

128. Job Satisfaction

Job satisfaction, also known as employee satisfaction, is a measure of how happy employees are with their jobs, whether they like the job or specific components of it, such as the nature of the work or supervision. Job satisfaction has cognitive, emotional, and behavioural components that may be quantified. Job satisfaction has been characterized in a variety of ways.

However, the most-used definition of job satisfaction in organizational research is that of Locke (1976), who described job satisfaction as "a pleasurable or positive emotional state resulting from the appraisal of one's job or job experiences" (p. 1304). Hulin and Judge (2003) expanded on this notion, stating that work satisfaction encompasses a wide range of psychological reactions to one's employment, including cognitive (evaluative), affective (or emotional), and behavioural components. In the organizational literature, several ideas on the causes of work satisfaction have been offered. These theories may be roughly categorized into three groups: 1. Situational theories claim that job happiness is influenced by the nature of one's employment or other factors in the workplace. 2. Dispositional methods, which claim that work happiness is based on an individual's personological composition. 3. Interactive theories claim that job happiness is the consequence of the interaction of situational and personality elements (EID and LARSEN, 2008).

129. Job Commitment

Organizational commitment is defined as an individual's psychological attachment to the organization in organizational behaviour and industrial and organizational psychology. Organizational scientists have also devised a slew of sophisticated definitions of organizational commitment, as well as a slew of measures to assess it. Allen and Meyer (1990) identified three essential aspects of organizational commitment. As the three aspects of organizational commitment, emotional, continuance, and normative, are included. Affective commitment, according to him, is defined as an employee's emotional attachment to, identification with, and participation in the company. The continuation component refers to an employee's commitment based on the expenses associated with leaving the company. The employee's sense of responsibility to stay with the company is referred to as the normative component.

130. Job Involvement

Job participation is the degree to which a person cognitively connects with his or her career. A person with a high degree of job engagement receives a lot of pleasure from their employment.

Job involvement can be defined as "the psychological identification with one's work" as well as "the degree to which the job situation is central to the employee and his or her identity" (Lawler & Hall, 1970, pp. 310–311). Employees with a high level of job involvement are more likely to regard work as the centre of their self-concepts (Frone & Russell, 1995), and they are also more likely to increase their self-esteem through successful job performance (Burke, 1991) and the display of organizationally beneficial behaviours (Diefendorff, Brown, Kamin, & Lord, 2002). Many researchers have recognized job engagement as a significant predictor of employee attitudes and performance because this sort of job identification can meet personal psychological needs (Brown) (Pfeffer, 1994). Job design, according to Lawler (1992) and Pfeffer, can improve job participation. For example, according to Bass (1965), employees' job participation may rise when they believe they have more decision-making authority at work, make significant contributions to the company's success or failure, and control their own work speed. Allowing employees influence over work content (e.g., setting the speed of work, product quality, and job skills and tools) might inspire employees to become more involved in their jobs, according to Blauner (1964).

131. Job-Related Burnout

Job burnout is a sort of work-related stress that manifests as a condition of physical or emotional tiredness, as well as a sense of diminished accomplishment and a loss of personal identity. "Burnout" is not a medical term. Other diseases, such as depression, are thought to be the cause of burnout, according to some specialists. Burnout, which is described as a sustained response to chronic emotional and interpersonal pressures on the job, may have a negative impact on a worker's health, motivation, and job performance, as well as jeopardize an organization's reputation by increasing employee turnover (Burke & Richardsen, 1993; Cordes & Dougherty, 1993; Maslach, Schaufeli, & Leiter, 2001). Burnout is described as a bad work-related state of mind that persists over time (Schaufeli and Enzmann, 1998). Burnout has previously been seen as a result of prolonged stress at work, which may be caused by a variety of factors such as high workload, role conflict and ambiguity, and a lack of engagement and social support (Shirom, 2003). There are various theories of job-related burnout, but they all start with the notion that a misalignment between a motivated employee's goals and values and reality in unfavourable working conditions leads to burnout via dysfunctional coping mechanisms (Schaufeli and Enzmann, 1998). Burnout has three qualitative components, according to the most often used operationalization: weariness, cynicism, and a lack of professional efficacy (Schaufeli et al., 1996).

132. Motivation

Employee motivation is defined as an inner and internal urge to exert the necessary effort and take action in work-related tasks. Money was seen as the essential input into the creation of products and services in the early twentieth century (Kreitner, 1995). However, it was discovered after a series of studies, one of which was known as the "Hawthorne Studies," conducted by Elton Mayo at the Hawthorne Works of the American Western Electric Company in Chicago from 1924 to 1932, that employees were not solely motivated by money, but that their behaviour was linked to their attitudes (Dickson, 1973, in Lindner, 1998). The Hawthorne experiments ushered in the human relations approach to management, in which managers prioritize employee needs and motivation (Bedeian, 1993).

This cleared the door for new ideas and definitions of workplace motivation and performance. Numerous definitions of motivation have been proposed in various academic areas, spanning from management to psychology to associated sciences. Motivation is derived from the Latin word "movere," which means "to move," according to Kreitner and Kinicki (1998) and Ramlall (2004). According to Butkus and Green (1999), motivation is derived from the term "motivate," which also means "to move, urge, or convince to act in order to fulfil a need." Motivation is described as "a decision-making process through which an individual selects desired objectives and initiates the behaviours necessary to achieve them" (Huczynski & Buchanan,1991, in Dartey-Baah, 2010). Motivation, according to Lindner (2004), is a psychological process that provides behaviour meaning, purpose, and direction. "Willingness to expend high amounts of effort toward organizational goals, conditioned by the effort's potential to satisfy some individual need," according to Robbins (2005). Motivation, according to Shah and Shah (2010), is the act of encouraging individuals to work hard, either individually or in groups, in order to get the greatest outcomes.

133. Job performance

Job performance determines whether or not a person does a good job. Human resources management includes job performance, which is researched academically as part of industrial and organizational psychology. Organizational outcomes and success are heavily influenced by performance.

134. Intention to leave/Intention to Quit/ Turnover Intention

The term 'intention to quit' simply refers to a worker's desire to leave his or her current employer. This idea is sometimes confused with the phrase "turnover intention," however the desire to depart is not the same as defining real turnover. The intention of an employee to freely change occupations or organizations is referred to as "turnover intention."

Staff retention and turnover are two major challenges that have a variety of consequences for businesses. In this regard, it's worth quoting Andrew Carnegie, the famed 19th-century entrepreneur, who said: "Take away my factories, my plants; take away my railroads, my ships, my transportation, take away my money; strip me of all of these but leave me my key employees, and in two or three years, I will have them all again" (Gupta & Srivastava, 2007).

Furthermore, the research of Ahlrichs (2000) revealed the most undervalued costs of key personnel turnover for firms. There are two types of expenses associated with a turnover: visible and invisible costs. Leave capitalization, recruiting fees, reference checks, security clearance, temporary worker costs, relocation costs, formal training costs, and induction charges are all examples of visible turnover costs. Increased HR and payroll administration, lost productivity, and informal training is examples of hidden expenses. Missed deadlines, loss of organizational expertise, poor motivation as a result of overwork, customer loss, and chain reaction turnover are some of the other hidden costs. Another negative impact of turnover on the company is on employee-customer interactions. Long-tenured staff are more likely to create personal ties with consumers. These bonds serve as the foundation for a virtuous circle of mutually beneficial interactions between staff and consumers. As a result, employee retention has a beneficial impact on client satisfaction and, eventually, profitability (Rust, Stewart, Miller, & Pielack, 1996).

135. Workplace Cyberbullying

Any sort of harassment or bullying that occurs online or through the use of electronic devices is referred to as cyberbullying. It may take many various forms (including through social media platforms, texts, apps, and emails) and can involve things like uploading insulting photographs, sending offensive words or threats, or threatening to publish personal information online. People utilize technology responsibly, but some have decided to abuse it by injuring, degrading, shaming, and personally abusing others (Hinduja & Patchin, 2012b; Kowalski, Limber, & Agatston, 2008; Patchin & Hinduja, 2010).

This phenomenon has been termed cyberbullying, which has been defined as ''willful and repeated harm inflicted through the use of computers, cell phones, and other electronic devices'' (Hinduja & Patchin, 2009, p. 5, 2012a). Cyberbullying may be seen as more malicious than "off-line" (i.e., conventional or schoolyard) bullying in various respects, including the fact that the assaults can be more severe, frequent, unintentional, and harder to stop (Hinduja & Patchin, 2009). Cyberbullies, unlike conventional bullies, are not bound by geography or time. Some cyberbullies may operate under the guise of anonymity, allowing them to attack others at any time and from any location they choose (Kowalski et al., 2008).

136. Workplace cyber harassment

The phrase "internet harassment," often known as "cyberbullying," refers to the use of the Internet to bully, harass, threaten, or deliberately embarrass someone. It can include things like sending unsolicited and/or threatening e-mails, among other things. Encourage others to send the victim unsolicited and/or threatening e-mail or to send the victim an excessive amount of e-mail messages. Viruses are sent via e-mail (electronic sabotage). Disseminating rumours. Making online disparaging remarks about the victim. Directly sending negative signals to the victim. Impersonating the victim online by delivering a message that is provocative, contentious, or seductive causes others to react unfavourably to the victim. During a live conversation, harassing the victim. Abusing others online, notably on social networking platforms. Sending pornography or other explicit content to the victim with the intent to offend.

137. Deindividuation

Deindividuation is a phenomenon in which people act irrationally, defiantly, and sometimes violently in situations where they believe they can't be personally identified (e.g., in groups and crowds and on the Internet). In the 1950s, American social psychologist Leon Festinger created the word "deindividuation" to characterize situations in which people cannot be individuated or detached from others. Because persons who are disguised inside a group cannot be easily found or blamed for their behaviour, some deindividuated conditions might lessen accountability. As a result, deindividuation's consequences are frequently regarded as socially undesirable.

138. Self-Perception

Self-perception is a person's perception of himself or any of the mental or physical characteristics that make up the self. Genuine self-awareness or varying degrees of distortion may be present in such a viewpoint. Also known as self-perception. Daryl Bem established the self-perception theory, which is a hypothesis of attitude creation. It claims that people form their attitudes by monitoring their own conduct and deducing which attitudes are responsible for it. Self-perception is the image we have of ourselves and our characteristics, as well as the judgments we make about them. Our self-concept, or the image we have in our brains of who we are, and our self-esteem, or how we rate and evaluate those attributes, are two key perceptual processes.

139. Stigma

A mark of shame linked with a specific incident, quality, or person is known as stigma. People believe that if something has a stigma associated with it, it is something to be embarrassed by. Social Stigma: Disapproval of, or prejudice against, an individual or group based on perceivable social features that help to separate them from other members of a society is referred to as social stigma.

140. Mental illness

Mental diseases are illnesses that cause changes in emotion, thought, or behaviour (or a combination of these). Distress and/or issues functioning in social, job, or family activities are common symptoms of mental diseases. Work is beneficial to one's mental health, yet a toxic workplace can lead to physical and mental health issues. Harassment and bullying at work are regular complaints, and they may have a significant negative impact on mental health.

Organizations may adopt a variety of practical steps to boost mental wellness in the workplace, which may also benefit productivity.

141. Backbiting

Backbiting affects almost everyone who works in an office environment, no matter where they are on the globe. Saying hurtful or nasty words about someone who isn't there is known as backbiting. And, let's be honest, almost everyone has engaged in backbiting at some point, whether as a listener or as the speaker. Employees who backstab and talk are an issue in offices all around the world. Even if you aren't the target, you may not enjoy hearing hurtful jokes about your coworkers or the poisonous environment that these remarks generate.

142. Backstabbing

Backstabbing happens when the target feels they have been purposely stabbed in the back and have experienced personal or professional injury, according to Malone and Hayes. Backstabbers at work come in a variety of shapes and sizes, including Put-downs, insulting statements, and derogatory remarks are hurled by belittlers. Credit thieves are those who take your ideas and then claim credit when a project succeeds. When a project goes bad, finger points assign responsibility to others. Rumour mongers incite hysteria by disseminating gossip, falsehoods, and half-truths that smear people's reputations. Slackers who avoid duty and delegate responsibilities to others. When they feel threatened by intellect and talent, scorched-earth bosses will undercut or even terminate a clever, talented employee.

143.   Tyrannical Behaviour

When you call someone a tyrant, you're implying that they're harsh or unjust to the individuals over whom they have power. A tyrannical ruler has unlimited power and authority, which he or she frequently exercises in an unfair, harsh, or oppressive manner. A tyrannical ruler has unlimited power and authority, which he or she frequently exercises in an unfair, harsh, or oppressive manner. The term tyrannical was first used in the 1530s, and it comes from the late-14th-century word tyranny, which comes from the Greek word "tyrannos", which means "master." Tyranny is the polar opposite of democracy, which places authority in the hands of the people, with the majority making the choices.

144.   Paranoia and suspicion

Paranoia is the unreasonable and persistent belief that others are 'out to get you' or that you are the object of others' constant, invasive scrutiny. This irrational fear of others can make it difficult for a person suffering from paranoia to operate socially or maintain intimate relationships. The Spectrum of Paranoid Workplace Behaviour Paranoid thinking may appear as an off-handed or weird remark that is disregarded as a misheard remark or a momentary period of strangeness. However, the remarks frequently persist, especially when people are under pressure, causing anxiety and dread among coworkers and bosses.

145. Lacklustre Employees

Employees that are unmotivated are likely to perform poorly as a result. Employees that are uninterested in their jobs provide poor customer service and put forth limited effort. Poor performance compels their coworkers to pick up the slack, which is an unjust burden that you should not put up with. Before you go after disgruntled personnel, take a look at the company's operations. It's critical to ensure that employees who are underperforming have been given a fair chance to succeed. Ascertain that the appropriate tools, support, and training have been provided to the targeted person. This includes ensuring that they are in roles that are a good fit for their skills and experience.

146. Deflecting Blame/ Behaviour

People employ deflecting as a psychological defence strategy to avoid taking responsibility for their actions. When they deflect, they're attempting to make themselves feel better about their mistakes. This is most likely related to previous experiences of getting into trouble for minor infractions. When you deflect anything, such as criticism or attention, you act in such a manner that it is not aimed at you or has no effect on you.

145. Abusive Deflection

Narcissists are frequently abusive verbally. They can even be physically abusive at times. It may be impossible to help this sort of narcissist cease deflecting while interacting with them. They may require expert assistance.

146. Dysfunctional Team Behaviour

A dysfunctional team is one that persistently underperforms due to a lack of professional or desirable collaboration and teamwork. One of the biggest challenges contributing to a loss of performance is conflicts that arise in teams and between team members, yet resolving them can be challenging. These basic dysfunctional behaviour patterns are usually a sign of one or more of the five major issues listed below. Patrick Lencioni characterized the five dysfunctions of a team in his 2002 book The Five Dysfunctions of a Team as a lack of trust, fear of confrontation, lack of commitment, avoidance of accountability, and inattention to outcomes.

147. Abusive Supervision

"Subordinates' judgments of the amount to which their supervisors engage in the persistent exhibition of hostile verbal and nonverbal actions" is how abusive supervision is characterized. Sustained demonstrations of nonphysical types of animosity performed by supervisors against their direct reports are referred to as abusive supervision. Public denigration, undermining, and explosive outbursts are examples of behaviours that come within the abusive supervision content area. Epper (2000, p. 186) stated, "subordinates whose supervisors were more abusive reported higher turnover, less favourable attitudes toward the job, life, and organization". Stress and conflict levels, deep-level dissimilarity, emotional intelligence, and histories of family undermining were all found as supervisor-level precursors of abusive supervision in numerous new research (Burton,

Hoobler, & Scheuer, 2012; Harris et al., 2011; Kiazad et al., 2010; Kiewitz et al., 2012; Tepper et al., 2011; Xiaqi et al., 2012).

148.   Aggressive Behaviour

Aggression in the workplace can be subtle or overt, but it is always a concern. Employees that behave aggressively create discomfort to people around them, lower morale, and can even result in the loss of employees or customers, as well as harming the company's brand and badly impacting the bottom line. Aggression is defined as any action or act aiming at injuring a person or animal or causing bodily damage, according to social psychology. Here are a few examples of aggressive behaviour: physical acts of violence, yelling, screaming, using obscene words, chatting about a coworker or spreading rumours about a coworker

Aggressive behaviour was described by Baron (1977: 7) as 'any form of behaviour directed toward the goal of harming or injuring another living being who is motivated to avoid such treatment.' Similarly, Berkowitz (1993: 3) refers to aggressive behaviour as 'any form of behaviour that is intended to injure someone physically or psychologically.' In a more recent study, Andersson and Pearson (1999) define aggression as deviant behaviour with intent to harm (p. 456). They contrast it with phrases like aggression, deviant conduct, antisocial behaviour, and incivility, which are all near-synonyms. Andersson and Pearson (1999) add to the evidence that most workplace aggressiveness takes the form of verbal rather than physical aggression, is passive rather than active, is indirect rather than direct, and is subtle rather than overt (Baron & Neuman, 1996).

149.   Politics and Political Behaviour

Organizational politics, according to most studies, refers to the complex mix of power, influence, and interest-seeking behaviours that control people's activities at work. Organizational politics, according to Ferris, Fedor, Chachere, and Pondy (1989a), is a social influence process in which behaviour is purposefully structured to optimize short-term or long-term self-interest. As they pointed out, self-interest might be in line with or at odds with the interests of others. Organizational politics may result in favourable or poor job outcomes as a result of these factors. Randolph (1985), for example, claimed that politics isn't necessarily bad; it's just a tool that people may use for the sake of the organization or for personal advantage. Kumar and Ghadially (1989) concluded in another study that organizational politics is both beneficial and damaging to members of the organization. Career progression, recognition and prestige, increased power and position, attainment of personal goals, getting the job done, feeling accomplished, increased sense of control, and success are all good results of politics. Loss of strategic power and position credibility, unpleasant attitudes toward others, internal feelings of guilt, and hindered work performance of many types are all negative results.

150. Job Distress

Job stress is described as the negative physical and emotional reactions that occur when the job demands do not meet the worker's talents, resources, or needs. Workplace stress can result in ill health and even harm. Stress responses are natural responses to external or internal disturbances that might be considered adaptive. When stress is intense, sustained, or both, it causes distress. Organizational politics may cause work dissatisfaction and burnout, as well as a positive and direct link between job dissatisfaction and violent conduct. Physical and emotional, interpersonal, attitudinal, and behavioural effects of occupational anxiety and burnout, according to Cordes and Dougherty (1993). These divisions can be narrowed into two key constructs according to Selye's (1975) typology: (1) physiological outcomes and (2) behavioural findings. First, work dissatisfaction and burnout can lead to serious medical problems. Maslach and Jackson (1981: 99–101) cited a number of physical complaints, including frequent headaches, prolonged colds, backaches, gastrointestinal disorders, and so on. However, and more importantly for this study, occupational strain and burnout may have an impact on people's real behaviour. People who are under a lot of stress at work may become jittery and impulsive or exhibit considerably less tolerant conduct.

151. Unethical Behaviour

Unethical workplace behaviour is **any action at work that goes against the prevailing moral norms of a community**. At work, unethical behaviour can take multiple forms and have multiple targets. (aggressive, spreading gossip, lying, jealousy, withholding effort, or even being absent without a valid justification). Unethical behaviour can be defined as actions that are against social norms or acts that are considered unacceptable to the public. Ethical behaviour is the complete opposite of unethical behaviour.

Ethical behaviour follows the majority of social norms, and such actions are acceptable to the public. Unethical behaviour in the workplace, although not always illegal, can harm a company's reputation resulting in loss of business, customers, employees, and possible closure of the company. Unethical behaviour is not unique to a specific industry or location and happens in all types of organizations and industries.

Kidwell & Martin (2005: 7) argued that deviant activities at work are unethical because "individuals who engage in these activities clearly lack moral strength and violate ethical standards". Drawing inferences from the previous definition, unethical workplace behaviour is defined here as behaviours that violate moral norms of working that are typically endorsed by the larger community. For example, taking excessive breaks, losing important work documents and acting rudely towards others that generally hamper work quality, quantity and property across organizations are all considered instances of unethical workplace behaviours (e.g. Kish-Gephart, Harrison & Treviño, 2010).

152. Perception of organizational justice/injustice

Corporate social responsibility focuses on the fairness of treatment of entities outside the organization, whereas organizational justice relates to perceptions of fairness in the treatment of individuals within the organization. Employees' perceptions of fairness in workplace procedures, interactions, and outcomes are referred to as 'organisational justice.' Justice is defined as an action or choice that is deemed morally correct based on ethical, religious, fairness, equity, or legal considerations (Pekurinen et al., 2017). It's a huge source of anxiety for both employers and employees (Swalhi et al., 2017). Employee perceptions of fairness inside an enterprise are referred to as organizational justice (Greenberg, 1990; Asadullah et al., 2017). Equity theory gave birth to the concept of organizational justice (Adams, 1963, 1965). It was advised that people compare their own perceived job outputs to their own perceived work inputs with their counterparts' similar ratios. As a result, their engagement in organizations can be altered (Colquitt et al., 2001). Time and effort are considered inputs, whereas benefits, such as promotions, income, recognition, equipment, or any other job-related resources, are considered outputs (Ghosh et al., 2017).

153. Corruption

Corruption is a dishonest and criminal technique for persons in positions of power to participate in unethical and illegal behaviour. They will do so solely to benefit themselves. As a result, they take unfair advantage of others. Incidental, institutional, and systemic corruption are all terms used to describe corruption. Small-scale embezzlement and misappropriation, bribes, favouritism, and prejudice are examples of incidental corruption (Kpundeh, 1998). Bribery and bribes, conspiracy to cheat, large-scale embezzlement, theft through public tender or disposal of public property, or economic benefits provided to privileged interests are all examples of institutional corruption (Kpundeh, 1998). Large-scale embezzlement via phantom workers on government payrolls, embezzlement of government funds via fake procurement, large-scale transfer of public property to special and privileged interests, and favours owing to political contributions are all examples of systemic corruption (Kpundeh, 1998).

154. Favouritism

In the workplace, favouritism refers to **a situation where someone in a leadership position demonstrates favour toward one employee over others**. This is usually unrelated to their job performance and instead occurs due to a personal bond of friendship shared between the two. According to Morettini, "Favouritism is part of human nature. No two people interact similarly to any other two, so it's impossible for all organization relationships to be "equal". It's only natural to gravitate to people with that you share common interests with, and with whom you have an easy rapport" (2006: 1). We can view favouritism from two perspectives: subordinate perceptions of supervisor favouritism or actual favouritism behaviours. According to the Merit Systems Protection Board, "favouritism occurs when human capital decisions are based on personal feelings and/or relationships and NOT on objective criteria, such as assessments of ability, knowledge, and skills" (2011: 1). supervisors use subjective criteria in hiring decisions, promotional decisions, performance evaluations, and work and task assignment decisions rather than objective measures. "Subjectivity opens the door to favouritism, where supervisors act on personal preferences toward subordinates to favour some subordinates over others" (Prendergast & Topel, 1996: 958). According to Dr Sayani Basu, "in the workplace, favouritism can be said when someone-or perhaps a group of people appears to be treated better than others and not necessarily for reasons related to superior work performance" (2009:1). In Duran and Morales approach to favouritism, "preferred individuals are those who belong to the group of friends of the organization. The unfairness that characterizes favouritism is found in the fact that decision-makers consciously favour their friends at the expense of someone else who is more deserving" (2009:3). According to Bassman and London, "showing favouritism may be abusive in itself, especially if the "out-group" subordinates are regularly excluded from opportunities for development, valued job assignments, pay increases, or other rewards" (1993:21). The use of favouritism in supervisor decision-making has limited academic literature in relation to ethical decision-making theory, leader-member exchange theory, or expectancy theory.

155. Humiliation

An act of humiliation is a type of punishment that is meant to make someone feel humiliated. Individuals who have been subjected to the most humiliating and public humiliations typically feel hopeless, helpless, and suicidal. Humiliation is described as an act of disgrace, embarrassment, or shame directed at another person. Humiliation causes a person great pain and has a mental impact. Bullying in the workplace has grown increasingly widespread. Employee engagement has been demonstrated to be negatively impacted by incivility, according to research.

156. Yelling

A loud cry or shout is used to address someone or something. A screaming culture may spread quickly in any organization, but it eventually makes people feel disengaged and unproductive. Supervisors and managers are legally permitted to yell at employees. When the yelling is directed at or against a protected group, however, it may be considered harassment.

157. Teasing

Teasing has a variety of meanings and applications. Teasing can take three different forms in human interactions: amusing, cruel, and educational. Depending on how it is employed and the desired result, teasing can have a range of outcomes. (1) When teasing is undesirable, it may be construed as harassment or mobbing, particularly in the workplace and at school, as well as bullying or emotional abuse. As teasing grows more common in a group, the lines between acceptable and unacceptable behaviour are blurred, and the behaviour becomes increasingly unpleasant. What began as harmless teasing can quickly escalate into workplace bullying or harassment. Reddy, V. (1991). Playing with others' expectations: Teasing and mucking about in the first year. (pp. 143-158) Basil Blackwell, Cambridge, MA

158.   Fatal Flaw

A fatal fault is a character flaw that eventually leads to a person's demise. In most cases, the word fatal fault suggests that the character is heroic and wonderful in other ways and that the fatal flaw itself might have been admirable in a different situation. A fatal fault is a serious flaw in a leader that affects more than just his or her effectiveness. A person with a fatal fault was never one of the organization's most effective leaders.

The degree to which a person is curious, original, intelligent, creative, and open to new ideas is referred to as openness. People who have a high level of openness appear to thrive in settings that involve flexibility and the ability to learn new things. They are eager to learn new abilities and perform well in training situations (M. R. Barrick and M. K. Mount,1991).

159.   Conscientiousness

The degree to which a person is structured, systematic, punctual, goal-oriented, and trustworthy is referred to as conscientiousness. Conscientiousness is the only personality trait that consistently predicts how well a person would succeed in a wide range of industries and jobs (M. R. Barrick and M. K. Mount, 1991).

160.   Extraversion

The degree to which a person is outgoing, talkative, gregarious, and enjoys socializing is known as extraversion. One of the well-established conclusions is that they are more effective in sales-related jobs (M. R. Barrick and M. K. Mount, 1991).

161. Agreeableness

The degree to which a person is affable, tolerant, sensitive, trustworthy, kind, and warm is referred to as agreeableness. To put it another way, persons who have a high level of agreeableness are pleasant and get along with others. Unsurprisingly, agreeable people continuously support others at work; this helping conduct is independent of their mood (R. Ilies, B. A. Scott, and T. A. Judge, 2006).

162. Neuroticism

The degree to which a person is anxious, irritable, temperamental, and moody is referred to as neuroticism. It's the only one of the Big Five dimensions where a high score isn't desirable. Neurotic people are more likely to have emotional adjustment issues and to be stressed and depressed on a regular basis. People with high levels of neuroticism have a variety of issues at work. They struggle to build and sustain connections, for example and are less likely to be sought out for guidance and friendship Klein, K. J., L. Beng-Chong, J. L. Saltz, and D. M. Mayer (2004).

163. Catfishing

According to (Chandler and Munday, 2020) "Catfishing is a deceitful practice in which someone fabricates a false identity or fictional persona on a social networking site, typically with the intention of preying on a specific victim". In today's social media age, catfishing is a major issue. Catfishers are much more than capable of committing crimes and harassing their victims nowadays. Catfishing is mostly used to steal identities, make victims dependent on the catfishers, and steal money. Catfishers use social networking platforms like Facebook, Tinder, Instagram, and others to carry out suspicious activities. They might ask for money, hunt for a sexual connection online, or simply waste your time by talking about romantic things that will never happen in person. The majority of catfishers are skilled manipulators and deceivers. They scrutinize their victims for vulnerable areas that they may exploit. They make a lot of promises and portray themselves in a flawless manner to get attention and confidence. Catfishing is a widespread problem in many workplaces. Sexual harassment in the workplace can have a substantial negative influence on a worker's well-being. When a person is harassed at work, their performance suffers dramatically, and most employees are unable to function effectively in these situations. The entire workplace inquiry should be coordinated to recognize a catfisher. Employee investigations should be conducted by management to identify workers who are catfishing at work. This inquiry must collect all information on the staff and their behaviour. Managers must cover all components, from using social media to employing professional communication tools.

164. Positive Organizational Behaviour

"The study and application of positively oriented human resource strengths and psychological capacities that can be measured, developed, and effectively managed for performance improvement in today's workplace," according to Luthans (2002b) (p. 59). Aside from optimism, it must also match the following requirements to be classified as a psychological resource capability under this established POB framework: (a) The capacity must be based on theory and research and validly measurable, and (b) it must be "state-like" (i.e., open to change and development) and have a demonstrated performance impact (Luthans, 2002a, 2002b; Luthans, Youssef, et al., 2007). Positive psychology does not claim to have discovered the value of optimism in people's lives.

Positive affectivity (PA), positive reinforcement, procedural justice, work satisfaction and commitment, prosocial and organizational citizenship activities, core self-evaluations, and many more positive notions have been identified in organizational research throughout the years. Instead, positive psychology, and its application to the workplace as POB, only tries to re-emphasize the value of a positive mindset (rather than a revolution or paradigm change).

165. Hope

Hope is described as "a positive motivational state that is built on an interactively formed feeling of effective (1) agency (goal-directed energy) and (2) routes (planning to fulfil objectives)" according to Snyder's (2000) theory of development and research (Snyder, Irving, & Anderson, 1991: 287). Hope's agency or "willpower" component, according to this definition, offers the resolve to attain objectives, whilst its routes or "way power" component supports the building of alternate roads to replace those that may have been obstructed in the pursuit of those goals. Hope has been demonstrated to be useful and related to performance in a variety of settings, including the workplace (Adams et al., 2002; Curry, Snyder, Cook, Ruby, & Rehm, 1997; Luthans, Avolio, Walumbwa, & Li, 2005; Luthans & Jensen, 2002; Luthans, Van Wyk, & Walumbwa, 2004; S. J. Peterson & Luthans, 2003; Snyder, 1995b; Youssef & Luthans, 2006). Importantly, both dispositional and state hope is acknowledged in the literature, and they are measured differently (Snyder, 2000; Snyder et al., 1996). Setting ambitious "stretch" goals, contingency planning, and regulating as required are all practical techniques for creating hope (Luthans, Avey, et al., 2006; Snyder, 2000).

166.   Resilient Behaviour

"The preservation of positive adjustment under stressful settings" is how resilient behaviour is defined. Employee and organizational resilience help businesses to adopt new learning techniques, implement new routines, and make better use of their resources in unpredictable times. Employee resiliency is defined as the capacity to adapt to changing circumstances. The organizational context, which includes leadership and organizational culture, aids this capacity. This suggests that companies have a significant impact on their employees' ability to change and perform under pressure. Employee resilience also has beneficial spillover effects: resilient individuals are better able to deal with problems outside of work, and organizations may improve community resilience by encouraging employee resilience. Employee resilience, as described by Näswall et al. (2013), is based on organizational resilience, which is defined as "a result of an organization's overall situation awareness, management of keystone vulnerabilities, and adaptive ability in a complex, dynamic, and linked environment" (McManus, Seville, Vargo, & Brunsdon, 2008, p. 82). Employee resilience is conceptualised as an "employee capability, facilitated and supported by the organisation, to utilize resources to continually adapt and flourish at work, even if/when faced with challenging circumstances." This entails competent management and the ability to overcome adversity or crisis while working in an often unknown area in order to achieve organizational goals (Seville, Brunsdon, Dantas, Le Masurier, Wilkinson, & Vargo, 2006). This concept reflects Luthans' (2002) description of resilience as a "developable ability" rather than a stable personality feature, as prior theorizations claimed (cf. Wagnild & Young, 1993).

167. Minimalist Personality

Minimalism is a philosophy that emphasizes deliberate living, i.e., living with only what you need and discarding the rest. It's about being content with what you have rather than what you lack. It's conceivable that you're already a minimalist without realizing it. A minimalist is someone who strives for simplicity, utility, and clarity. They live a lifestyle that emphasizes what they value in life – what makes them happy – rather than material stuff. They aren't distracted by non-essentials and instead concentrate on what is genuinely important to them.

168. Optimistism

Optimism is a positive mental state marked by optimism and confidence in one's ability to succeed and have a bright future. Optimism is a steady personality characteristic that is associated with good aspirations for the future. Optimists believe that good things will happen to them, whilst pessimists believe that awful things will happen to them (Scheier & Carver, 1985). Optimism is a state of mind that expresses a belief or hope that the outcome of a single attempt, or the outcome of all endeavours, will be positive, beneficial, and desirable. A glass half full or half empty is a frequent phrase used to depict optimism vs pessimism. An optimist views the glass as half full, while a pessimist sees the glass as half empty. The phrase comes from the Latin word optimal, which means "best." Optimism is defined as expecting the best possible outcome from any given scenario in the traditional definition of the word. In psychology, this is referred to as dispositional optimism. As a result, it expresses a conviction that future circumstances will turn out well. As a result, it is seen as a character characteristic that promotes stress resilience.

169. Pessimism

Pessimism is defined by the American Psychological Association as "the attitude that things will go wrong and that people's wishes or aims are unlikely to be fulfilled. A pessimistic personality has a more negative—or, as some could say, realistic—approach to life. Pessimistic refers to a person's attitude of constantly expecting the worse. A gloomy outlook isn't particularly hopeful, doesn't display much optimism, and can be a downer for others. Pessimism refers to the belief that evil outweighs good and that negative things are more likely to occur. Pessimistic refers to a person's attitude of constantly expecting the worse. A gloomy outlook isn't particularly hopeful, doesn't display much optimism, and can be a downer for others.

Pessimism refers to the belief that evil outweighs good and that negative things are more likely to occur. Pessimists are, by definition, pessimistic. According to the Merriam Webster dictionary, the definition of pessimism definition is "an inclination to emphasize adverse aspects, conditions, and possibilities or to expect the worst possible outcome." And according to dictionary.com, the definition is "the tendency to speak, anticipate, or emphasize only bad or undesirable outcomes, results, conditions, problems, etc." A pessimist is someone who always perceives the negative aspects of a situation. They find it difficult to believe that things will turn out. They see the world through a half-empty rather than a half-full lens. Many pessimists feel that by constantly expecting the worse, they are protecting themselves. They think that if they assume the worst from the beginning, they will not be disappointed when it occurs, and they live their lives accordingly.

170. Cynicism

Cynics in the workplace doubt their leaders' motivations and feel that, if given a chance, their bosses will take advantage of their efforts (Kanter and Mirvis, 1989). The high incomes paid to business CEOs contribute to scepticism (Wilhelm, 1993). Employee cynicism is a state of mind marked by dissatisfaction, pessimism, and disappointment, as well as scorn for and scepticism of corporate organizations, CEOs, and/or other workplace things. Employee cynicism is defined as unfavourable attitudes of irritation, disappointment, and disdain for and distrust of businesses, CEOs, supervisors, and other workplace items (Andersson, 1996; Dean et al.,

1998). Employee cynicism is defined by Dean, Brandes, and Dharwadkar (1998) in a review paper as "a negative attitude toward one's employing firm, composed of" Employee cynicism is defined by Dean, Brandes, and Dharwadkar (1998) in a review paper as "a negative attitude toward one's employing firm, which has three dimensions: 1. a conviction that the organization is untrustworthy 2. a negative attitude toward the organization; and 3. a proclivity to engage in disparaging and critical conduct toward the organization in line with these attitudes and feelings. Longer working hours, work intensification, inadequate leadership and management, new workplace arrangements, and the constant shrinking and delayering of organizations have all been offered as new paradigms of employee-employer relations (Bunting, 2004; Feldman, 2000). Employee cynicism is defined by Dean, Brandes, and Dharwadkar (1998) in a review paper as "a negative attitude toward one's employing firm, which has three dimensions: 1. a conviction that the organization is untrustworthy 2. a negative attitude toward the organization; and 3. a proclivity to engage in disparaging and critical conduct toward the organization in line with these attitudes and feelings. Longer working hours, work intensification, inadequate leadership and management, new workplace arrangements, and the constant shrinking and delayering of organizations have all been offered as new paradigms of employee-employer relations (Bunting, 2004; Feldman, 2000).

References

A. M. Ryan (Eds.), Personality and work: Reconsidering the role of

Adams, J. S. (1965). Inequity in social exchange. In L. Berkowitz (Ed.), Advances in experimental social psychology (Vol. 2, pp. 267–299). New York: Academic Press.

Allen , K. , Blascovich , J. , & Mendes , W.B . (2002). Cardiovascular reactivity and the presence of pets, friends, and spouses: Th e truth about cats and dogs . Psychosomatic Medicine, 64 , 727 – 739 .

Altheide, D. L., Adler, P. A., Alder, P., & Altheide, D. A. (1978). The social meanings of employee theft. In J. M. Johnson & J. D. Douglas (Eds.), Crime at the top: Deviance in business and the professions. Philadelphia, PA: J. B. Lippincott.

Amabile, T. M. & Gitomer, J. (1984) Children's artistic creativity: Effects of choice in task materials. Personality and Social Psychology Bulletin, 10, 209-215.

Amabile, T. M. (1983). Social psychology of creativity: A componential conceptualization. Journal of Personality and Social Psychology, 45, 997-1013.

American Psychological Association. (2009).Stress in America 2009.Washington, DC: Author.

Andersson, L., & Pearson, C. (1999). Tit for tat? The spiralling effect of incivility in the workplace. Academy of Management Review, 24, 452–471. doi:10.5465/ amr.1999.2202131.

Anxiety and Depression Association of America. (2006). Workplace stress & anxiety disorders survey. Retrieved from http://www.adaa.org/workplace-stress-anxiety-disorders-survey

Aquino, K., & Douglas, S. 2003. Identity threat and anti-social behaviour in organizations: the moderating effects of individual differences, aggressive modeling, and hierarchical status. Organizational Behaviour and Human Decision Processes, 90(1): 195-208.

Aquino, K., & Lamertz, K. (2004). A relational model of workplace victimization: Social roles and Methodological review of harassment research 243]. Patterns of victimization in dyadic relationships. 1023 1034. Journal of Applied Psychology 89 – doi:10.1037/0021-9010.89.6.102.

Aquino, K., & Thau, S. (2009). Workplace victimization: Aggression from the target's perspective. Annual Review of Psychology, 60, 717-741.

Aronsson, G., Gustafsson, K., & Dallner, M. (2000). Sick but yet at work. An empirical study of sickness presenteeism. Journal of Epidemiology and Community Health, 54, 502–509.

Ashforth, B. (1994). Petty tyranny in organizations. Human Relations, 47, 755–778.

at the Annual Meeting of the Academy of Management, Dallas, TX.

Avolio, B. J., Walumbwa, F. O., & Weber, T. J. 2009. Leadership: Current theories, research, and future directions. In Annual review of psychology, vol. 60: 421– 449. Palo Alto, CA: Annual Reviews

Awadh, A.M. & Wan Ismail, W. (2012). The impact of personality traits and employee work-related attitudes on employee performance with the moderating effect of organizational culture: the case of

Saudi Arabia, Asian Journal of Business and Management Sciences, 1(10), 108-127.

Back, M. D. , Baumert, A. , Denissen, J. J. A. , Hartung, F. , Penke, L. , Schmukle, S. C. , Schönbrodt, F. D. , … Wrzus, C. (2011). PERSOC: A unified framework for understanding the dynamic interplay of personality and social relationships. European Journal of Personality, 25, 90–107. https://doi.org/10.1002/per.811.

Bakker, A.B., Hetland, J., Olsen, O.K. and Espevik, R. (2019), "Daily strengths use and employee wellbeing: the moderating role of personality", Journal of Occupational and Organizational Psychology, Vol. 92 No. 1, pp. 144-168.

Baltimore, J.J. (2006). Nurse collegiality: Fact or fiction. Nursing Management, 37(5), 28-36.

Bandura, A. (2001). Social cognitive theory: An agentic perspective. *Annual review of psychology* (Vol. 52, pp. 1-26). Palo Alto: Annual Reviews, Inc.

Bandura, A. 1977. Social learning theory. Prentice Hall, Englewood Cliffs, New Jersey, USA

Barmby, T., Ercolani G. and Treble, J.G. (2002), "Sickness Absence: an International Comparison", Economic Journal, 112(480), pp. 315-331.

Barrick, M.R., & Mount, M.K. (1991). The big five personality dimensions and job performance: A meta-analysis. Personnel Psychology, 44, 1-26.

Bassman, E., & London, M. (1993). Abusive managerial behaviour. Leadership & Organization Development Journal, 14(2), 18.

Basu, S. (2009). Work Place Nepotism and Stress. SSRN Electronic Journal. doi:10.2139/ssrn.1409089.

Bateman, T. S., & Organ, D. W. (1983). Job satisfaction and the good soldier: The relationship between affect and employee "citizenship." Academy of Management Journal, 26, 587–595.

Baumeister, R. F. (Ed.). (1993). *Self-esteem: The puzzle of low self-regard.* Plenum Press. https://doi.org/10.1007/978-1-4684-8956-9

Beer, A., & Brooks, C. (2011). Information quality in personality judgment: The value of personal disclosure. *Journal of Research in Personality, 45*(2), 175–185.

Bennett, R.J. and Robinson, S.L. (2000) Development of a measure of workplace deviance. Journal of Applied Psychology, 85, 349-360.

Benoliel, B., 2022. *What's Your Conflict Management Style? | Walden University.* [online] Waldenu.edu. Available at: <https://www.waldenu.edu/news-and-events/walden-news/2017/0530-whats-your-conflict-management-style> [Accessed 25 May 2022].

Bensman, J. and Gerver, J. (1963) Crime and punishment in the factory: The function of deviancy in maintaining the social system. American Sociological Review, 28, 588- 598.

Berkowitz, L. (1993). Aggression: Its causes, consequences and control. New York: McGraw-Hill.

Berkowitz, L., & Daniels, L. (1963) Responsibility and dependency. Journal of Abnormal and Social Psychology, 66, 429-437.

Bernard, N. S., Dollinger, S. J., & Ramaniah, N. V. (2002). Applying the big five personality factors to the impostor phenomenon. Journal of Personality Assessment, 78(2), 321-333.

Bindl U and Parker SK (2011) Feeling good and performing well? Psychological engagement and positive behaviors at work. In: Albrecht S (ed.) Handbook of Employee Engagement: Perspectives, Issues, Research and Practice. Cheltenham: Edward Elgar, 385–398.

Bock, G. W., & Ho, S. L. (2009). Non-work related computing (NWRC). Communications of the ACM, 52, 124–128.

Britt, T. W., & Jex, S. M. (2008). Organizational psychology: A scientist-practitioner approach.

Bunting, Madeleine. 2004. Willing Slaves: How the Overwork Culture is Ruling our Lives. London: Harper Collins.

Burton JP, Hoobler JM, Scheuer ML. 2012. Supervisor workplace stress and abusive supervision: the buffering effect of stress. J. Bus. Psychol. 27:271–79

Bycio, P. (1992), "Job performance and absenteeism: a review and meta-analysis", Human relations, 45, pp. 192-220.

Campbell, D. T. (1965) Ethnocentric and other altruistic motives. In D. Levine (Ed.), Nebraska symposium on motivation (pp. 283-311). Lincoln: University of Nebraska Press.

Campbell, J. P. (1990). Modeling the performance prediction problem in industrial and organizational psychology. In M. D. Dunnette & L. M. Hough (Eds.), *Handbook of industrial and organizational psychology* (2nd ed., Vol. 1, pp. 687–732). Palo Alto, CA: Consulting Psychologists Press.

Chandra, G., & Robinson, S. L. (2009, August). They're talking about me again: The negative impact of being the target of gossip. Paper presented at the 2009 Academy of Management Annual Meeting, Chicago, Illinois, USA.

Chandler, D. and Munday, R., 2020. A Dictionary of Media and Communication. Oxford: Oxford University Press, Incorporated.

Chapman, LS. (2005). Presenteeism and its role in worksite health promotion. Am J Health Promot 2005;19(4):1-8.

Chaput, April, "The Impact of the Use of Favoritism on Work Groups" (2012). Seminar Research Paper Series. Paper 36.

Cheng, J. L. (1983). `Organizational context and upward in¯uence: An experimental study in the use of power tactics', Group and Organizational Studies, 8, 337 – 355.

  Chikotas, N. E., Parks, C. and Olszewski, K. (2007) 'Occupational Safety and Health Objectives of Healthy People 2010: A Systematic Approach for Occupational Health Nurses—Part I', AAOHN Journal, 55(2), pp. 65–72. doi: 10.1177/216507990705500204.

Christie & F. Geis (Eds.), Studies in Machiavellianism (pp. 163-172). New York: Academic Press.

Christie, R., & Geis, F. (1970a). Studies in Machiavellianism. New \brk: Academic Press. Christie, R., & Geis, F. (1970b). The ten dollar game. In R.

Clance, P. R. (1985). The Impostor Phenomenon: Overcoming the fear that haunts your success. Atlanta, GA: Peachtree. Clance, P. R., Dingman, D., Reviere, S. L., & Stober, D. R. (1995). Impostor Phenomenon in an interpersonal/social context: Origins and treatment. Women and Therapy, 16(4), 79-96.

Clance, P. R., & Imes, S. A. (1978). The impostor phenomenon in high achieving women: Dynamics and therapeutic intervention. Psychotherapy: Theory, Research, and Practice, 15(3), 241–247.

Clance, P. R., & O"Toole, M. A. (1988). The impostor phenomenon: An internal barrier to empowerment and achievement. Women and Therapy, 6(3), 51-64.

Colligan, T. and Higgins, E., 2006. Workplace Stress. *Journal of Workplace Behavioural Health*, 21(2), pp.89-97.

Cooper, A., Safir, M. P., & Rosenmann, A. (2006). Workplace worries: A preliminary look at online sexual activities at the office – emerging issues for clinicians and employers. CyberPsychology & Behavior, 9, 22–29.

Cordes, C. L., & Dougherty, T. W. (1993). A review and an integration of research on job burnout. Academy of Management Review, 18, 621–656.

Cortina, L. M., Magley, V. J., Williams, J. H., & Langhout, R. D. (2001). Incivility in the workplace: Incidence and impact. Journal of Occupational Health Psychology 6 , , 64–80. doi:10.1037/ 1076-8998.6.1.64.

Cressey, D. (1953) Other People's Money: A Study in the Social Psychology of Embezzlement. Belmont, CA: Wadsworth.

Cressey, D. R. (1953). Other people's money: A study of the social psychology of embezzlement. Belmont, CA: Wadsworth.

Crino, M. D. (1994). Employee sabotage: A random or preventable phenomenon? Journal of Managerial Issues, 6, 311–330.

Curry, L.A., Snyder, C.R., Cook, D.L., Ruby, B.C. and Rehm, M., 1997. Role of hope in academic and sport achievement. *Journal of personality and social psychology*, 73(6), p.1257.

Danziger, J. N. (2008b). On cyberslacking: Workplace status and personal Internet use at work. CyberPsychology & Behavior, 11, 287–292.

Day, D. V., & Kilduff, M. (2003). Self-monitoring personality and work

Day, D. V., & Kilduff, M. (2003). Self-monitoring personality and work relationships: Individual differences in social networks. In M. R. Barrick & A. M. Ryan (Eds.), Personality and work: Reconsidering the role of personality in organizations (pp. 205–228). San Francisco: Jossey–Bass.

de Gouveia, C. D., Van Vuuren, L. V., & Crafford, A. (2005). Towards a typology of gossip in the workplace. Journal of Human Resource Management, 3(2), 56–68.

Dean Jr, J.W., Brandes, P. and Dharwadkar, R., 1998. Organizational cynicism. *Academy of Management review, 23*(2), pp.341-352.

Deci, E. L., & Ryan, R. M. (1985a). The general causality orientation scale: Self-determination and personality. *Journal of Research in Personality, 19*, 109–134.

Deci, E. L., & Ryan, R. M. (1985b). *Intrinsic motivation and self-determination in human behavior*. New York: Plenum Press.

Diduck, A., N. Bankes, D. Clark, and D. Armitage. 2005. Unpacking social learning in social-ecological systems: case studies of polar bear and narwhal management in northern Canada. In F. Berkes, R. Huebert, H. Fast, M. Manseau, and A. Diduck, editors. Breaking ice: renewable resource and ocean management in the Canadian North. Northern Light Series, Arctic Institute of North America and University of Calgary Press, Calgary, Alberta, Canada.

Dionne, G. and Dostie, B. (2007), "New evidence on the determinants of absenteeism using linked employer-employee data", Industrial & Labor Relations Review 61 (1), pp. 108-120.

Duffy, M. K., Ganster, D. C., & Pagon, M. (2002). Social undermining in the workplace. Academy of Management Journal 45, 331 351. doi: 10.2307/3069350.

Dunbar, R. I. M. (2004). Gossip in evolutionary perspective. *Review of General Psychology, 8*(2), 100–110. https://doi.org/10.1037/1089-2680.8.2.100

Duran, M., & Morales, A. (2009). The Economics of Favoritism, 1–10.

Einarsen, S., Hoel, H., Zapf, D., & Cooper, C. L. (Eds.) (2011). Bullying and harassment in the workplace: Developments in theory, research and practice . Boca Raton, FL: CRC Press.

Ellwardt, L., Labianca, G., & Wittek, R. (2012). Who are the objects of positive and negative gossip at work? A social network perspective on workplace gossip. Social Networks, 34(2), 193-205

Fehr, B., Samson, D., & Paulhus, D. L. 1992. The construct of Machiavellianism: Twenty years later. In C. Spielberger & J. Butcher (Eds.), Advances in personality assessment Vol. 9: 77-116. Hillsdale, NJ: Lawrence Erlbaum.

Ferris, D. L., Brown, D. J., Berry, J. W. & Lian, H. (2008). The development and validation of the workplace ostracism scale. Journal of Applied Psychology, 93, 1348–1366. 10.1037/a0012743

Ferris, D. L., Brown, D. J., Berry, J. W., & Lian, H. 2008. The development and validation of the workplace ostracism scale. Journal of Applied Psychology, 93: 1348-1366

Ferris, G. R., & Kacmar, K. M. (1989). Perceptions of organizational politics. Paper presented at the 49th Annual Academy of Management Meeting, Washington, D.C.

Fischhoff, B., Lichtenstein, S., Slovic, P., Derby, S. L., & Keeney, R. L. (1981). Acceptable risk. Cambridge, England: Cambridge University Press.

Fox, S. & Stallworth, L. E. (2005). Racial/ethnic bullying: Exploring links between bullying and racism in the US workplace. Journal of Vocational Behavior, 66, 438–456. 10.1016/j.jvb.2004.01.002

from conduct disorder to antisocial personality disorder following treatment to adolescent substance abuse. American

Gangestad, S. W., & Snyder, M. (2000). Self-monitoring: Appraisal and reappraisal. *Psychological Bulletin, 126*(4), 530–555. https://doi.org/10.1037/0033-2909.126.4.530

Garrett, R. K., & Danziger, J. N. (2008a). Disaffection or expected outcomes: Understanding personal Internet use during work. Journal of Computer-Mediated Communication, 13, 937–958. Garrett, R. K., &

Gecas, Viktor, and Michael L. Schwalbe. 1983. "Beyond the Looking-glass Self: Social Structure and Efficacy-Based Self-Esteem." Social Psychology Quarterly 46:77–88.

Gerber, A., Huber, G., Doherty, D. and Dowling, C., 2011. The Big Five Personality Traits in the Political Arena. Annual Review of Political Science, 14(1), pp.265-287.

Giacalone, R. A., & Jurkiewicz, C. L. (2003). Handbook of workplace spirituality and organizational performance. Armonk, NY: M.E. Sharpe

Giacalone, R.A. & Greenberg, J. (1997). Antisocial behavior in organizations. Thousand Oaks, CA: Sage.

Gouldner, A. (1960) The norm of reciprocity: A preliminary statement. American Sociological Review, 25, 161-178.

Gouldner, A.W. (1954) Wildcat Strike: A Study in WorkerManagement Relationships. New York: Harper and Row.

Greenberg, J. (1990), "Looking fair versus being fair: management impressions of organizational justice", in Staw, B.M. and Cummings, L.L. (Eds), Research in Organizational Behavior and Develop.

Greengard, S. (2001). Gossip poisons business– HR can stop it. Workforce, 80(7), 24-28.

Gruter, M. & Masters, R. D. (1986). Ostracism as a social and biological phenomenon: An introduction. Ethology and Sociobiology, 7, 149–158. 10.1016/0162-3095(86)90043-9.

Gunnthorsdottir, A., McCabe, K., & Smith, V. 2002. Using the Machiavellianism instrument to predict trustworthiness in a bargaining game. Journal of Economic Psychology, 23: 49-66.

Hall, D. T. (2002). Careers in and out of organizations. Thousand Oaks, CA: Sage.

Hall, D. T., & Chandler, D. E. (2005). Psychological success: When the career is a calling. Journal of Organizational Behavior, 26, 155-176.

Hamachek, D. E. (1978). Psychodynamics of normal and neurotic perfectionism. *Psychology: A Journal of Human Behavior, 15*(1), 27–33.

Heneman, R. L., & Werner, J. M. (2005). Merit Pay: Linking Pay To Performance In A Changing World (2nd edition). Greenwich, CT: Information Age Publishing.

Henry, S. (1978b) Crime at work: The social construction of amateur property theft. Sociology, 12, 245- 263.

Herskovits, M. J. (1955). Cultural Anthropology, Knopf, NY.

Heslin, P.A., & Klehe, U.C. (2006). Self-efficacy. In S. G. Rogelberg (Ed.), Encyclopedia of Industrial/Organizational Psychology (Vol. 2, pp. 705-708). Thousand Oaks: Sage.

Hewett, R., Liefooghe, A., Visockaite, G. and Roongrerngsuke, S. (2018), "Bullying at work: cognitive appraisal of negative acts, coping, well-being, and performance", Journal of Occupational Health Psychology, Vol. 23 No. 1, pp. 71.

Horning, D.N.M. (1970) Blue collar theft: Conceptions of property, attitudes toward pilfering, and work group norms in a modern industrial plant. In E.O. Smigel and H.L. Ross (eds), Crimes against Bureaucracy (pp. 46±64). New York: Van Nostrand Reinhold.

House, R. J. 1977. A 1976 theory of charismatic leadership. In J. G. Hunt & L. L. Larsen, (Eds.), Leadership: The cutting edge: 189 – 207. Carbondale: Southern Illinois University Press.

Hsiao YT, et al. (2016) Practical Guidelines for Incorporating Knowledge-Based and Data-Driven Strategies into the Inference of Gene Regulatory Networks. *IEEE/ACM Trans Comput Biol Bioinform* 13(1):64-75

https://doi.org/10.1111/j.1744-6570.1998.tb00743.x

Hulin, C. (1991). Adaptation, persistence, and commitment in organizations. In M. D. Dunnette & L. M. Hough (Eds.), *Handbook of industrial and organizational psychology* (pp. 445–505). Consulting Psychologists Press.

Ilies, R., Scott, B. A., & Judge, T. A. 2006. The interactive effects of personal traits and experienced states on intraindividual patterns of citizenship behavior. Academy of Management Journal, 49: 561-575.

Ingham, A. G., Levinger, G., Graves, J., & Peckham, V. (1974). The Ringelmann effect: Studies of group size and group performance. Journal of Experimental Social Psychology, 10, 371-384.

Irwin, F. W. (1953). Stated expectations as a function of probability and desirability of outcomes. Journal of Personality, 21, 329–335.

Ison, R., N. Roling, and D. Watson. 2007. Challenges to science and society in the sustainable management and use of water: investigating the role of social learning. Environmental Science & Policy 10:499-511.

Jex, S. and Britt, T., 2008. *Organizational Psychology*. Hoboken: John Wiley & Sons.

Jex, S. M. (1998).Stress and job performance: Theory, research, and implications for managerial practice. Thousand Oaks, CA: SAGE.

Johnson, P. R., & Indvik, J. (2004). The organizational benefits of reducing cyberslacking in the workplace. Journal of Organizational Culture, Communications, and Conflict, 8, 55–62.

Journal of Psychiatry, 155, 479–485.

Kanter, D.L. and Mirvis, P.H., 1989. *The cynical Americans: Living and working in an age of discontent and disillusion*. Jossey-Bass.

Kaplan, R. and Kaiser, R., 2009. *Stop Overdoing Your Strengths*. [online] Harvard Business Review. Available at:

<https://hbr.org/2009/02/stop-overdoing-your-strengths> [Accessed 21 April 2022].

Katz, D., and R.L. Kahn. 1966. Organizations and the system concept. The social psychology of organizations. New York: John Wiley & Sons, Inc.

Katz, D., and R.L. Kahn. 1978. The social psychology of organizations. New York: Wiley.

Keen, M., T. Bruck, and R. Dyball. 2005b. Social learning: a new approach to environmental management. Pages 3-21 in M. Keen, V. Brown, and R. Dyball, editors. Social learning in environmental management: towards a sustainable future. Earthscan, London, UK.

Keen, M., V. A. Brown, and R. Dyball. 2005a. Social learning in environmental management: towards a sustainable future. Earthscan, London, UK.

Kerr S, Jermier JM. 1978. Substitutes for leadership: their meaning and measurement. Organ. Behav. Hum. Perform. 22:376–403.

Kiazad K, Restubog SLD, Zagenczyk TJ, Kiewitz C, Tang RL. 2010. In pursuit of power: the role of authoritarian leadership in the relationship between supervisors' Machiavellianism and subordinates' perceptions of abusive supervisory behavior. J. Res. Pers. 44:512–19.

Kidwell, R. E., & Martin, C. L. (2005). The prevalence (and ambiguity) of deviant behavior at work. In: R. E. Kidwell & C. L. Martin (Eds), Managing organizational deviance (pp. 1–21). Thousand Oaks, CA: Sage.

Kiewitz C, Restobug SLD, Zagenczyk TJ, Scott KD, Garcia PRJM, Tang RL. 2012. Sins of the parents: selfcontrol as a buffer between supervisors' previous experience of family undermining and subordinates' perceptions of abusive supervision. Leadersh. Q. 23:869–82

Kish-Gephart, J. J., Harrison, D. A., & Treviño, L. K. (2010). Bad apples, bad cases, and bad barrels: Meta-analytic evidence about sources of unethical decisions at work. Journal of Applied Psychology, 95(1), 1-31. doi: 10.1037/a0017103.

Klein, K.J., Lim, B.C., Saltz, J.L. and Mayer, D.M., 2004. How do they get there? An examination of the antecedents of centrality in team networks. *Academy of Management Journal, 47*(6), pp.952-963.

Kniffin, K. M., & Sloan Wilson, D. (2010). Evolutionary perspectives on workplace gossip: Why and how gossip can serve groups. *Group & Organization Management, 35*(2), 150–176. https://doi.org/10.1177/1059601109360390.

Kpundeh S (1999) The fight against corruption in Sierra Leone. In: Stapenhurst R, Kpundeh S (eds) Curbing Corruption: Toward a Model for Building National Integrity. World Bank, District of Columbia, pp. 207-234.

Kumar, P. & Ghadially, R. (1989). Organizational politics and its effect on members of organizations. Human Relations. 42: 305-314.

Kundi, Y., Aboramadan, M., Elhamalawi, E. and Shahid, S., 2020. Employee psychological well-being and job performance: exploring mediating and moderating mechanisms. *International Journal of Organizational Analysis*, 29(3), pp.736-754.

Latane, B., & Darley, J. (1970) The unresponsive bystander: Why doesn't he help? New York: Appleton-Century-Crofts.

Leary, M. R., Kowalski, R. M., Smith, L. & Phillips, S. (2003). Teasing, rejection, and violence: Case studies of the school shootings. Aggressive Behavior, 29, 202–214. 10.1002/ab.10061

Lehman, W. E., & Simpson, D. D. (1992). Employee substance use and on-the-job behaviors. *Journal of Applied Psychology, 77*(3), 309–321. https://doi.org/10.1037/0021-9010.77.3.309.

Lencioni, P. M. (2002). *The five dysfunctions of a team.* Jossey-Bass.

Lim, S., & Cortina, L. (2005). Interpersonal mistreatment in the workplace: The interface and impact of general incivility and sexual harassment. Journal of Applied Psychology, 90, 483–496. doi:10.1037/0021-9010.90.3.483

Lim, V. K. G., & Chen, D. J. Q. (2012). Cyberloafing at the workplace: Gain or drain on work? Behaviour & Information Technology, 31(4), 343–353. https://doi.org/10.1080/01449290903353054

Lim, V. K. G., & Teo, T. S. H. (2005). Prevalence, perceived seriousness, justification and regulation of cyberloafing in Singapore: An exploratory study. Information and Management, 42, 1081–1093.

Lim, V. K. G., & Teo, T. S. H. (2009). Mind your E-manners: Impact of cyber incivility on employees' work attitude and behavior. Information Management, 46, 419–425.

Lim, V. K. G., & Teo, T. S. H. (2009). Mind your E-manners: Impact of cyber incivility on employees' work attitude and behavior. Information & Management, 46(8), 419–425.

Luthans, F. and Jensen, S.M., 2002. Hope: A new positive strength for human resource development. *Human resource development review*, *1*(3), pp.304-322.

Luthans, F. and Youssef, C.M., 2007. Emerging positive organizational behavior. *Journal of management*, *33*(3), pp.321-349.

Luthans, F., & Youssef-Morgan, C. M. (2017). Psychological capital: An evidencebased positive approach. Annual Review of Organizational Psychology and Organizational Behavior, 4, 339–366.

Luthans, F., 2002. The need for and meaning of positive organizational behavior. *Journal of Organizational Behavior: The International Journal of Industrial, Occupational and Organizational Psychology and Behavior*, *23*(6), pp.695-706.

Luthans, F., 2002. The need for and meaning of positive organizational behavior. *Journal of Organizational Behavior: The International Journal of Industrial, Occupational and Organizational Psychology and Behavior*, *23*(6), pp.695-706.

Luthans, F., Avey, J. B., Avolio, B. J., Norman, S. M., & Combs, G. M. (2006). Psychological capital development: Toward a micro-intervention. *Journal of Organizational Behavior, 27*(3), 387–393. https://doi.org/10.1002/job.373

Luthans, F., Van Wyk, R. and Walumbwa, F.O., 2004. Recognition and development of hope for South African organizational leaders. *Leadership & Organization Development Journal*.

Mao, Y., Liu, Y., Jiang, C. and Zhang, I., 2017. Why am I ostracized and how would I react? — A review of workplace ostracism research. *Asia Pacific Journal of Management,*.

Mars, G. (1973) Chance, punters and the fiddle: Institutionalized pilferage in a hotel dining room. In M. Warner (ed.), The Sociology of the Workplace (pp. 200±210). New York: Halsted Press.

Martocchio, J. J., & Harrison, D. A. (1993). To be there or not be there? Questions, theories, and methods in absenteeism research. Research in Personnel and Human Resources Management, 11, 259-328.

Martucci, W. C., & Sinatra, K. R. (2009). Antibullying legislation—a growing national trend in the new workplace. Employment Relations Today, 35, 77-83.

Maslach, C., & Jackson, S. E. (1981). The measurement of experienced burnout. Journal of Occupational Behavior, 2, 99–113.

Mastrangelo, P. M., Everton, W., & Jolton, J. A. (2006). Personal use of work computers: Distraction versus destruction. CyberPsychology & Behavior, 9, 730–741.

Matthews G, Clance PR. Treatment of the impostor phenomenon in psychotherapy clients. Psychotherapy in Private Practice. 1985; 3(1): 71-81.

McCarthy, J. M., Trougakos, J. P., & Cheng, B. H. (2016). Are anxious workers less productive workers? It depends on the quality of social exchange. Journal of Applied Psychology, 101,279–291. http://dx.doi.org/10.1037/apl0000044

McHoskey, J. (2001). Machiavellianism and sexuality: On the moderating role of biological sex. Personality and Individual Differences, 31, 779–789. McHoskey, J. (1995). Narcissism and Machiavellianism. Psychological Reports, 77, 755–759.

McHoskey, J. W. 1999. Machiavellianism, intrinsic versus extrinsic goals, and social interest: A self-determination theory analysis. Motivation & Emotion, 23: 267-283.

McLeod, S., 2017. Stanford prison experiment. *Simply Psychology*.

McManus, S., Seville, E., Vargo, J. and Brunsdon, D., 2008. Facilitated process for improving organizational resilience. *Natural hazards review*, 9(2), pp.81-90.

Michelson, G., & Mouly, V. S. (2004). Do loose lips sink ships? The meaning, antecedents and consequences of rumour and gossip in organizations. Corporate Communications, 9(3), 189–201.

Mills, J. E., Hu, B., Beldona, S., & Clay, J. (2001). Cyberslacking! A wired-workplace liability issue. Cornell Hotel and Restaurant Administration Quarterly, 42, 34–47.

Mirvis, P. and Kanter, D.L., 1989. Combating cynicism in the workplace. *National Productivity Review*, 8(4), pp.377-394.

Mor Barak, M. E. (2000). Beyond affirmative action: Toward a model of diversity and organizational inclusion. Administration in Social Work, 23, 47–68.

Mor Barak, M. E., & Cherin, D. A. (1998). A tool to expand organizational understanding of workforce diversity: Exploring a measure of inclusion-exclusion. Administration in Social Work, 22, 47–64.

Morettini, P. (2006, October 21). Favoritism in the workplace--How to avoid even the perception of it. Articlesbase. Retrieved from http://www.articlesbase.com/non-fictionarticles/favoritism-in-the-workplacehow-toavoid-even-the-perception-of-it-65657.html.

Motowidlo, S. J., Packard, J. S., & Manning, M. R. (1986). Occupational stress: Its causes and consequences for job performance. Journal of Applied Psychology, 71,618–629. http://dx.doi.org/10.1037/0021-9010.71.4.618

Mount, M.K. and Barrick, M.R. (1998) Five Reasons Why the "Big Five" Article Has Been Frequently Cited. Personnel Psychology, 51, 849-857.

Mousa, M., Massoud, H.K. and Ayoubi, R.M. (2020), "Gender, diversity management perceptions, workplace happiness and organisational citizenship behaviour", Employee Relations: The International Journal, Vol. 1.

Mruk, C. J. (1995). *Self-esteem: Research, theory, and practice.* Springer Publishing Co.

Mumford, M. D., & Gustafson, S. B. (1988). Creativity syndrome: Integration, application, and innovation. *Psychological Bulletin, 103*(1), 27–43. https://doi.org/10.1037/0033-2909.103.1.27.

Myers, M. G., Stewart, D. G., & Brown, S. A. (1998). Progression

Namie, G. (2003). Workplace bullying: escalated incivility. Ivey Business Journal, 68, pp. 1–6.

NANCY TUANA (2006). *The Speculum of Ignorance: The Women's Health Movement and Epistemologies of Ignorance. , 21(3), 1– 19.*doi:10.1111/j.1527-2001.2006.tb01110.x .

Näswall, K., Kuntz, J., Hodliffe, M. and Malinen, S., 2013. Employee resilience scale (EmpRes): Technical report.

Nembhard, I. M., & Edmondson, A. C. (2006). Making it safe: The effects of leader inclusiveness and professional status on psychological safety and improvement efforts in health care teams. Journal of Organizational Behavior, 27, 941–966.

Noon, M., & Delbridge, R. (1993). News from behind my hand: Gossip in organizations. *Organization Studies, 14*(1), 23–36. https://doi.org/10.1177/017084069301400103.

Organ, D. W. (1988). Organizational citizenship behavior: The good solider syndrome. Lexington, MA: Lexington Books.

Organizational politics and organizational support to employee attitudes and behavior'. Paper presented

Oswalt, B., Elliott-Howard, F., Austin, S. F. (2003). Cyberslacking—Legal and ethical issues facing IT managers. Paper presented at the annual conference of the International Association for Computer Information Systems. Las Vegas, NV

Owens, B. 2009 "Humility in organizational leadership." Unpublished doctoral dissertation, University of Washington, Seattle.

Owens, B. P., Johnson, M. D., & Mitchell, T. R. 2013. Expressed humility in organizations: Implications for performance, teams, and leadership. Organization Science, 24: 1517–1538.

Owens, B., and D. Hekman 2012 "Modeling how to grow: An inductive examination of humble leader behaviors, contingencies, and outcomes." Academy of Management Journal, 55: 787-818.

Pahl-Wostl, C. 2006. The importance of social learning in restoring the multifunctionality of rivers and floodplains. Ecology and Society 11(1): 10. [online] URL: http://www.ecologyandsociety.org/vol11/iss1/art10/.

Pahl-Wostl, C., and M. Hare. 2004. Processes of social learning in integrated resources management. Journal of Community and Applied Social Psychology 14:193-206.

Pahl-Wostl, C., E. Mostert, and D. Tàbara. 2008. The growing importance of social learning in water resources management and sustainability science. Ecology and Society 13(1): 24. [online] URL: http: //www.ecologyandsociety.org/vol13/iss1/art24/.

Pahl-Wostl, C., J. Sendzimir, P. Jeffrey, J. Aerts, G. Berkamp, and K. Cross. 2007b. Managing change toward adaptive water management through social learning. Ecology and Society 12(2): 30. [online] URL: http://www.ecologyandsociety.org/vol12/ iss2/art30/.

Pahl-Wostl, C., M. Craps, A. Dewulf, E. Mostert, D. Tàbara, and T. Taillieu. 2007a. Social learning and water resources management. Ecology and Society 12(2): 5. [online] URL: http://www.ecology andsociety.org/vol12/iss2/art5/.

Parker SK, Williams HM, Turner N. (2006). Modeling the antecedents of proactive behavior at work. Journal of Applied Psychology, 91, 636–652

Parker, S.K.; Collin, C.G. Taking stock: Integrating and differentiating multiple proactive behaviors. J. Manag. 2010, 36, 633–662.

Parson, E. A., and W. C. Clark. 1995. Sustainable development as social learning: theoretical perspectives and practical challenges for the design of a research program. Pages 428-60 in L. H. Gunderson, C. S. Holling, and S. S. Light, editors. Barriers and bridges to the renewal of ecosystems and institutions. Columbia University Press, New York, New York, USA.

Paulhus, D. L., & Williams, K. M. (2002). The dark triad of personality: Narcissism, Machiavellianism, and psychopathy. Journal of Research in Personality, 36, 556-563.

Paulhus, D. L., & Williams, K. M. (2002). The Dark Triad of personality: Narcissism, Machiavellianism and psychopathy. Journal of Research in Personality, 36, 556–563.

Pawar, B. S. (2008). Two approaches to workplace spirituality facilitation: A comparison and implications. Leadership & Organization Development Journal, 29, 544 –567. doi:10.1108/01437730810894195

Pee, L. G., Woon, I. M. Y., & Kankanhalli, A. (2008). Explaining non-work-related computing in the workplace: A comparison of alternative models. Information & Management, 45, 120–130.

personality in organizations (pp. 205–228). San Francisco: Jossey–Bass

Pinder, C. C. and Harlos, K. P. (2001). 'Employee silence: quiescence and acquiescence as responses to perceived injustice'. In Rowland, K. M. and Ferris, G. R. (Eds), Research in Personnel and Human Resources Management, Vol. 20. New York: JAI Press, 331–69.

Prendergast, C., & Topel, R. H. (1996). Favoritism in organizations. The Journal of Political Economy, 104(5), 958.

Proyer, René T., and Frank A. Rodden. 2013. "Is the Homo Ludens Cheerful and Serious at the Same Time? An Empirical Study of Hugo Rahner's Notion of Ernstheiterkeit." Archive for the Psychology of Religion 35:213–31.

Proyer, René T., and Nicole Jehle. 2013. "The Basic Components of Adult Playfulness and Their Relation with Personality: The

Hierarchical Factor Structure of Seventeen Instruments." Personality and Individual Differences 55:811–16.

Proyer, René T., and Willibald Ruch. 2011. "The Virtuousness of Adult Playfulness: The Relation of Playfulness with Strengths of Character." Psychology of Well-Being: Theory, Research, and Practice 1. Symons, Donald. 1979. The Evolution of Human Sexuality.

Pulakos, E. D., Arad, S., Donovan, M. A., & Plamondon, K. E. (2000). Adaptability in the workplace: Development of a taxonomy of adaptive performance. Journal of Applied Psychology, 85(4), 612–624. doi:10.1037//0021-9010.85.4.612.

R. Wheeler, "We all do it: Unconscious behavior, bias, and diversity," Law Libr. J., vol. 107, no. 2, pp. 15–36, 2015.

Ramingwong S, Ramingwong L. A tale behind mum effect. Int J Inf Syst Proj Manag [Internet]. 2013;1(3):47–58.

Randall, M., Cropanzano, R., Bormann, C. and Birjulin, A. (August, 1994). `The relationship of

Randolph, W. A. (1985). Understanding and managing organizational behavior. Homewood, IL: Richard D. Irwin.

Reddy, V., 1991. Playing with others' expectations: Teasing and mucking about in the first year.

Reed, M. S., E. D. G. Fraser, A. J. Dougill. 2006. An adaptive learning process for developing and applying sustainability indicators with local communities. Ecological Economics 59:406-418.

relationships: Individual differences in social networks. In M. R. Barrick

Ringelmann, M. (1913a). Appareils de cultur mecanique avec treuils et cables (resultats d'essais) [Mechanical tilling equipment with winches and cables (results of tests)]. Annales de I'lnstitut National Agronomique, 2e serie—tome XII, 299-343.

Ringelmann, M. (1913b). Recherches sur les moteurs animes: Travail de rhomme [Research on animate sources of power: The work of man]. Annales de I'lnstitut National Agronomique, 2e serie—tome XII, 1- 40.

Roberson, Q. M. (2006). Disentangling the meanings of diversity and inclusion in organizations. Group & Organization Management, 31, 212–236.

Robinson, P. R. Shaver, & L. S. Wrightsman (Eds.), Measures of personality and social psychological attitudes (pp. 373–412). San Diego, CA: Academic Press.

Robinson, S.L. and Bennett, R.J. (1995) A typology of deviant workplace behaviors: A multidimensional scaling study. Academy of Management Journal, 38, 555-572.

Robinson, S.L. and Greenberg, J. (1998) Employees behaving badly: Dimensions, determinants, and dilemmas in the study of workplace deviance. In D.M. Rousseau and C. Cooper (eds), Trends in Organizational Behavior (Vol. 5, pp. 1±30). New York: Wiley.

Robinson, S.L. and Greenberg, J. (1998) Employees behaving badly: Dimensions, determinants, and dilemmas in the study of workplace deviance. In D.M. Rousseau and C. Cooper (eds), Trends in Organizational Behavior (Vol. 5, pp. 1-30). New York: Wiley.

Rosenberg, Morris, Carmi Schooler, Carrie Schoenbach, and Florence Rosenberg. 1995. "Global Self-Esteem and Specific Self-Esteem." American Sociological Review 60:141–56.

Rosenberg, Morris. 1976. "Beyond Self-Esteem: The Neglected Issues in Self-concept Research." Paper presented at the annual meetings of the ASA.

Rospenda, K. M., & Richman, J. A. (2004). The factor structure of Generalized Workplace Harassment. , , 221 238.

Sackett, P. R., & DeVore, C. J. (2001). Counterproductive behaviors at work. In N. Anderson, D. Ones, H. Sinangil, & C. Viswesvaran (Eds.), Handbook of industrial, work, and organizational psychology, Vol. 1 (pp. 145164).

Sakulku, J. & Alexander, J. (2011). The imposter phenomenon. International Journal of Behavioral Science, 6(1), 73-92.

Salary.com. (2009). The 2008 wasting time at work survey reveals a record number of people waste time at work.

Schaubroeck, J. M., Shen, Y., & Chong, S. (2017). A dual-stage moderated mediation model linking authoritarian leadership to follower outcomes. Journal of Applied Psychology, 102, 203-214. doi: 10.1037/apl0000165.

Scheier, M.F. and Carver, C.S., 1985. Optimism, coping, and health: assessment and implications of generalized outcome expectancies. *Health psychology*, *4*(3), p.219.

Schwartz, S. H. (1994). Beyond individualism/collectivism: New cultural dimensions of values. In U. Kim, H. C. Triandis, C. Kagitcibasi, S. C. Choi, & G. Yoon (Eds.), Individualism and collectivism: Theory, methods, and applications (pp. 85–119). Thousand Oaks: Sage Publications.

Schwartz, S. H. (1999). A theory of cultural values and some implications for work. Applied Psychology: An International Review, 48(1), 12–47.

Scott, S. G., & Bruce, R. A. (1994). Determinants of Innovative Behavior: A Path Model of Individual Innovation in the Workplace. *The Academy of Management Journal*, *37*(3), 580–607. https://doi.org/10.2307/256701.

Scott, S.G., and Bruce, R.A. (1994), „Determinants of innovative behavior: A path model of individual innovation in the workplace", Academy of Management Journal, Vol. 37 No. 3, pp. 580-607.

Seville, E., 2008. Resilience: great concept but what does it mean?

S. Ramingwong and S. Snansieng, "A Survey on Mum Effect and Its Influencing Factors*," in ProjMAN -International Conference on Project Management*, Lisbon, Portugal, 2013.

Shamir, B., House, R. J., & Arthur, M. B. 1993. The motivational effects of charismatic leadership: A selfconcept based theory. Organization Science, 4: 577–594.

Sharma, P., Kong, T.T.C. and Kingshott, R.P.J. (2016), "Internal service quality as a driver of employee satisfaction, commitment and performance: exploring the focal role of employee well-being", Journal of Service Management, Vol. 27 No. 5, pp. 773-797.

Smith, C. A., Organ, D. W., & Near, J. P. (1983). Organizational citizenship behavior: Its nature and antecedents. Journal of Applied Psychology, 68, 653–663.

Snyder, C.R. ed., 2000. *Handbook of hope: Theory, measures, and applications*. Academic press.

Snyder, C.R., Harris, C., Anderson, J.R., Holleran, S.A., Irving, L.M., Sigmon, S.T., Yoshinobu, L., Gibb, J., Langelle, C. and Harney, P., 1991. The will and the ways: development and validation of an individual-differences measure of hope. *Journal of personality and social psychology, 60*(4), p.570.

Snyder, M. (1974). Self-monitoring of expressive behavior. *Journal of Personality and Social Psychology, 30*(4), 526–537. https://doi.org/10.1037/h0037039

Spector, P. E., & Fox, S. (2005). The stressor-emotion model of counterproductive work behavior (CWB). In S. Fox & P. E. Spector (Eds.), Counterproductive work behavior: Investigations of actors and targets (p. 46). Washington, DC: American Psychological Association.

Spector, P. E., Bauer, J. A., & Fox, S. 2010. Measurement artifacts in the assessment of counterproductive work behavior and organizational citizenship behavior: Do we know what we think we know? Journal of Applied Psychology, 95: 781.

Staempfli, Marianne B. 2007. "Adolescent Playfulness, Stress Perception, Coping, and Well- Being." Journal of Leisure Research 39:393–412.

Stamper, C.L. and Masterson, S.S. (2002), "Insider or outsider? How employee perceptions of insider

Stapenhurst, F. and S. J. Kpundeh (1998), "Public participation in the fight against corruption", Canadian journal of development studies, Vol. 19, No. 3.

Steele CM, Aronson J. 1995. Stereotype threat and the intellectual test performance of African Americans. J. Personal. Soc. Psychol. 69(5):797–811

Steg, L., & Vlek, C. (2009). Encouraging pro-environmental behaviour: An integrative review 889 and research agenda. Journal of Environmental Psychology, 29, 309-317. https://doi.org/10.1016/j.jenvp.2008.10.004.

Sun, L.-Y., Zhang, Z., Qi, J., & Chen, Z. X. (2012). Empowerment and creativity: A cross-level investigation. *The Leadership Quarterly, 23*(1), 55–65. https://doi.org/10.1016/j.leaqua.2011.11.005.

SYKES, Gresham M. [e] MATZA, David. (1957), "Techniques of Neutralization". American Sociological Review, Vol. 22, Dezembro, 1957.

Tàbara, J. D., and C. Pahl-Wostl. 2007. Sustainability learning in natural resource use and management. Ecology and Society 12(2): 3. [online] URL: http://www.ecologyandsociety.org/vol12/iss2/ art3/.

Tajfel, H. (1982), Social Identity and Intergroup Relations, Cambridge University Press, Cambridge.

Tajfel, H. and Turner, J.C. (1986), "The social identity theory of intergroup behaviour", in Worchel, S. and Austin, W.G. (Eds), Psychology of Intergroup Relations, Nelson-Hall, Chicago, IL, pp. 7-24.

Taylor, L. and Walton, P. (1971) Industrial sabotage: Motives and meanings. In S. Cohen (ed.), Images of Deviance (pp. 219±245). London: Penguin.

Tepper BJ, Moss SE, Duffy MK. 2011. Predictors of abusive supervision: supervisor perceptions of deep-level dissimilarity, relationship conflict, and subordinate performance. Acad. Manag. J. 54:279–94.

Tepper BJ. 2000. Consequences of abusive supervision. Acad. Manag. J. 43:178–90.

Tepper, B. J. (2000). Consequences of abusive supervision. , Academy of Management Journal 43, 178 190. doi:10.2307/1556375.

Tisu, L., Lups, a, D., Vîrga, D. and Rusu, A. (2020), "Personality characteristics, job performance and mental health the mediating role of work engagement", Personality and Individual Differences, Vol. 153.

Triandis, H. C. (1995). Individualism and collectivism. Boulder, CO: Westview.

Turban, D.B. and Yan, W. (2016), "Relationship of eudaimonia and hedonia with work outcomes", Journal of Managerial Psychology, Vol. 31 No. 6, pp. 1006-1020.

Turnley, W. H., & Bolino, M. C. (2001). Achieving desired images while avoiding undesired images: Exploring the role of self-monitoring in impression management. *Journal of Applied Psychology, 86*(2), 351–360. https://doi.org/10.1037/0021-9010.86.2.351

UBC News. 2022. *Workplace sabotage fueled by envy, unleashed by disengagement: UBC research.* [online] Available at: <https://news.ubc.ca/2011/10/06/workplace-sabotage-fueled-by-envy-unleashed-by-disengagement-ubc-research/> [Accessed 19 April 2022].

Vanderbleek, Linda, Edward H. Robinson III, Montserrat Casado-Kehoe, and Mark E. Young. 2011. "The Relationship between Play and Couple Satisfaction and Stability." The Family Journal 19:132–39.

Wagnild, G.M. and Young, H.M., 1993. Development and psychometric. *Journal of nursing measurement, 1*(2), pp.165-17847.

Weber, Marco, and Willibald Ruch. 2012. "The Role of Character Strengths in Adolescent Romantic Relationships: An Initial Study on Partner Selection and Mates' Life Satisfaction." Journal of Adolescence 35:1537–46.

Websense, Inc. Web@Work (2006).

Weinstein, N. D. (1980). Unrealistic optimism about future life events. Journal of Personality and Social Psychology, 39, 806–820.

Wells, L. E., & Marwell, G. (1976). Self-esteem: Its conceptualization and measurement. Beverly Hills, Calif: Sage Publications.

Willard, N. (2011). School response to cyberbullying and sexting: the legal challenges. Brigham Young University Education and Law Journal, 1, 75–125.

Williams, K. D. & Nida, S. A. (2009). Is ostracism worse than bullying? In M. J.Harris (Ed.), Bullying, rejection, and peer victimization: A social cognitive neuroscience perspective (pp. 279–296). New York, NY: Springer.

Williams, K. D. (2001). Ostracism: The power of silence. New York, NY: Guilford.

Williams, K. D. (2007). Ostracism. Annual Review of Psychology, 58, 425–452. 10.1146/annurev.psych.58.110405.085641

Williams, K. D. 2007. Ostracism. Annual Review of Psychology, 58: 425-452

Williams, K. D., Karau, S. J., & Bourgeois, M. J. (1993). Working on collective tasks: Social loafing and social compensation. In M. A. Hogg & D. Abrams (Eds.), Group motivation: Social psychological perspectives (pp. 130–148). Harvester Wheatsheaf.

Williams, S. & Cooper, C. L. (1998). Measuring occupational stress: Development of the pressure management indicator. Journal of Occupational Health Psychology, 3, 306–321. 10.1037/1076-8998.3.4.306.

Wills , T.A . (1991). Social support and interpersonal relationships . In M.S. Clark (Ed.), Prosocial behavior (pp. 265 – 289). Newbury Park, CA : Sage .

Wilson, D. S., Near, D., & Miller, R. R. 1996. Machiavellianism: A synthesis of the evolutionary and psychological literatures. Psychological Bulletin, 119: 285-299.

Woll, Stanley B. 1989. "Personality and Relationship Correlates of Loving Styles." Journal of Research in Personality 23:480–505.

Wu, L., Wei, L., & Hui, C. 2011. Dispositional antecedents and consequences of workplace ostracism: An empirical examination. Frontiers of Business Research in China, 5: 23-44.

Wylie, Ruth C. 1979. The Self-Concept: Theory and Research on Selected Topics. University of Nebraska.

Xiaqi, D., Kun, T., Chongsen, Y., & Sufang, G. (2012). Abusive supervision and LMX: Leaders' emotional intelligence as antecedent variable and trust as consequence variable. Chinese Management Studies, 6, 257–270.

Yarnal, Careen, and Xinyi Qian. 2011. "Older-Adult Playfulness: An Innovative Construct and Measurement for Healthy Aging Research." American Journal of Play 4:52–79.

Zigarmi, D., Galloway, F.J. & Roberts, T.P. Work Locus of Control, Motivational Regulation, Employee Work Passion, and Work Intentions: An Empirical Investigation of an Appraisal Model. J Happiness Stud 19, 231–256 (2018). https://doi.org/10.1007/s10902-016-9813-2